Satan's Ten Most Believable Lies

The Seattle School of Theology & Psychology
2501 Elliott Ave.
Seattle, WA 98121
theseattleschool.edu

WITHDRAWN

The Seattle School

10025987

WITHDRAWN

Satan's Ten Most Believable Lies

by

DAVE BREESE

MOODY PRESS

CHICAGO

To Lance and Virginia Latham,
whose godly concern and careful ministry
of the gospel of the grace of God
brought me to the Savior

© 1974 by
DAVE BREESE

Original title: *His Infernal Majesty*
Trade Paperback Edition, 1987

All rights reserved. No part of this book may be reproduced in any form without permission in writing from the publisher, except in the case of brief quotations embodied in critical articles or reviews.

All Scripture quotations, unless noted otherwise, are from the King James Version.

The use of selected references from various versions of the Bible in this publication does not necessarily imply publisher endorsement of the versions in their entirety.

Library of Congress Cataloging in Publication Data

Breese, Dave, 1926-
    Satan's ten most believable lies.

    Reprint. Originally published 1974 under title:
His Infernal Majesty.
    1. Devil.   I. Breese, David, 1926-   His
Infernal Majesty.   II. Title.
BT981.B67   1987   235'.47   86-28568
ISBN 0-8024-7675-9 (pbk.)

1 2 3 4 5 6 7 Printing/LC/Year 91 90 89 88 87

Printed in the United States of America

Contents

Preface

In the ministry of the gospel, I have had the happy opportunity to see the wonderful working of God in the lives of many. I have noted with concern the mounting activity of Satan as well. *Satan's Ten Most Believable Lies* was written out of increased concern that we, the Christians of our time, be not ignorant of his devices.

In the assembling of this material, I found myself increasingly grateful for the helpful insights of the many pastors, educators, and Christian leaders with whom I have had the opportunity to serve in the ministry of evangelism. They remain nameless out of reluctance on my part to connect anyone by implication to the views contained herein. By their very doctrinal nature, the following pages will evoke minus and plus reactions, and I will welcome considered comments or questions.

Our Christian Destiny secretarial staff played an important part in the preparation of this manuscript. My thanks goes to Ruth Friesen, who patiently typed several drafts. I am most grateful for those who have the talent and patience to turn longhand and dictation into readable words.

Finally, this book is offered with every prayer that it will be a useful instrument to aid in the deliverance of some from the dread machinations of its frightful subject.

Introduction

He began full of wisdom and perfect in beauty. As the brightest of the angels, he was given a position of power and influence in the universe second only to God Himself. His infernal majesty, Satan, was once Lucifer, the angel of light. Could we have seen him then, we would have been greatly tempted to fall down and worship him. Scripture says about him, "Thou wast perfect in thy ways from the day that thou wast created, till iniquity was found in thee" (Exodus 28:15).

The iniquity that was found in the heart of Lucifer produced the first rebellion in the history of the universe. With a heart that was lifted up with pride to the point of irrationality, he fancied that he could take over the throne of God and the leadership of all of creation. The prime minister aspired to be the King and was cast out of heaven. The moral history of the universe is the outgrowth of the original polarity between sin and righteousness, beween the Creator and the created.

The account of that rebellion is well known, being delineated for us by Isaiah and Ezekiel and other writers of Scripture. Satan was cast out of heaven to earth, and here he continues his dreadful machinations against the will of God. The most obvious activity of Prince Lucifer in our present age is that form of his activity that can be seen, his *overt* activity. As a consequence, even the public press is filled with accounts of Satan worship, witchcraft, occult practices, spiritism, pagan religious rites, and many other evidences of satanism. Millions are addicting themselves to fortune-telling, palmistry, astrology, and tarot cards. From cemetery seances to Ouija board parties, the story of the occult revival continues to grow. These viewable forms of satanic activity are frightening evidence that Prince Lucifer is continuing, even expanding, his work in our "modern" world.

There is, however, a form of satanic activity that is more deadly than witchcraft. Serious damage has been done in naive personalities because of overt spiritualist activity, but far greater havoc has been wrought by another kind of satanism, the covert production and propagation of false doctrine. The enemy has produced a significant triumph when he can spread in our society a broad set of false views about God, Christ, the Holy Spirit, sin, the purpose of life, and other imperative points of Christian doctrine. For every one person who is subverted by Satan worship, thousands are enmeshed in Satan's more deadly trap: doctrinal error. People who are otherwise perfectly rational, who would not dream of attending a seance, are, nevertheless, the more thoroughly undermined simply because they believe the wrong thing.

Satan's trafficking in false doctrine is more dangerous than spiritism. Few inquiries could then be more helpful than to examine the doctrines of Satan in the hope of deliverance from his mind-destroying theology.

1

More Deadly
than
Witchcraft

Satan carries on an activity more dangerous than witch-craft and more subversive than astrology. As terrifying as those practices may be, they will never compose his ulti-mate weapons. They are external. Witchcraft, for in-stance, is certainly dangerous, but it deceives only a few. Ouija boards, black magic, sorcery, and the like, lead to dreadful spiritual consequences, but their victims are lim-ited.

The most potentially rewarding activities of Satan —his deadliest influences—are not overt and public. Rather, the *covert*, the hidden, activities of the devil con-stitute his greatest accomplishment. With witchcraft, or-gies, séances, and demon possession, he has captured thousands. With false doctrine, he has subverted millions.

The dangers of these twin activities of his infernal majesty, the *overt* and the *covert,* are pointed out to us in a prophetic warning from the pages of the New Testament. The apostle Paul, in his letter to Timothy, carefully warns us, "Now the Spirit speaketh expressly, that in the latter times some shall depart from the faith, giving heed to se-ducing spirits, and doctrines of demons" (1 Timothy 4:1, NSRB*). Here the overt activity of the evil one is "se-ducing."

*New Scofield Reference Bible.

Seducing spirits lure some from the path of rectitude with the promise of physical ecstasy. Satan's representatives function as spiritual prostitutes, basically by appealing to the lust of the flesh, seducing the naive and the vulnerable to the point that they forsake their faith. Sex appeal with religious overtones is a diabolically clever one-two punch that Satan has thrown at the unwary.

The Bible gives us a telling description of those who combine sex appeal and false religious teaching.

> But false prophets also arose among the people, just as there will also be false teachers among you, who will secretly introduce destructive heresies, even denying the Master who bought them, bringing swift destruction upon themselves. And many will follow their sensuality, and because of them the way of truth will be maligned; and in their greed they will exploit you with false words; their judgment from long ago is not idle, and their destruction is not alseep. . . . especially those who indulge the flesh in its corrupt desires. . . . But these, like unreasoning animals, born as creatures of instinct to be captured and killed, reviling where they have no knowledge, will in the destruction of those creatures also be destroyed, suffering wrong as the wages of doing wrong. They count it a pleasure to revel in the daytime. They are stains and blemishes, reveling in their deceptions, as they carouse with you, having eyes full of adultery and that never cease from sin, enticing unstable souls, having a heart trained in greed, accursed children; forsaking the right way they have gone astray. . . . These are springs without water, and mists driven by a storm, for whom the black darkness has been reserved. For speaking out arrogant words of vanity they entice by fleshly desires, by sensuality, those who barely escape from the ones who live in error, promising them freedom while they themselves are slaves of corruption; for by what a man is overcome, by this he is enslaved. (2 Peter 2:1-3, 10, 12-15, 17-19, NASB*)

*New American Standard Bible

In the light of this Scripture, the function of witchcraft is revealed. Not quite so obvious but equally satanic is the role of the religious huckster who promotes a magic snake-oil version of pseudo-Christianity. Seducing spirits do the overt work of Satan.

Paul's warning to Timothy also notes the nature of the covert working of Satan. That deadly, hidden work is the production of "doctrines of demons." A doctrine is a categoric statement of belief. The use of the word *doctrines*, therefore, implies a satanic system of belief that appears to be categoric, appealing, and—worst of all—true. The production of attractive doctrinal falsehoods is the most deadly activity of the enemy of God in the world today.

Christ warned us that Satan was a liar from the beginning and the father of lies (John 8:44). At this point, we do well to remember that the cleverest liar makes statements that sound most nearly like the truth. The father of lies will surely present assertions that sound blessedly true and are only proved false when analyzed in depth. The most subtle created being in all the universe is Lucifer. The cleverest set of lies that he has ever produced is the satanic system of doctrine. With his doctrines, he presses quiet arguments upon reasonable men, appealing to high intelligence and mature sensibilities. Every person who is not a Christian believes one or another demonic doctrine as the first principle of his life. Many Christians, though saved by believing the truth, have been rendered spiritually impotent through accepting, along with the truth, a doctrine of Satan.

It is interesting and even titillating to consider the overt activities of Satan. It is surely of more value, however, to study the doctrines of the devil and the biblical answer to these frightening subversions. *Subversion*, incidentally, is a good word for all of this, for it literally means "to undermine the truth," or, "less than the truth." A proposition that is slightly less than the truth is a far more treacherous lie than the clenched fist of categoric denial.

An understanding of sound doctrine is the most important single form of knowledge for the Christian. In order to understand and refute the doctrines of the devil, we must first know sound, biblical doctrine. The apostle Paul admonished Timothy to give attendance to doctrine and to take heed continually to the importance of it, reminding him that this attention would save both him and his hearers. Few activities could be more valuable on the part of the church of Christ than a return to the careful study of biblical doctrine. It is the necessary prelude to prayer, more important than "experience" and any other aspect of the Christian life. Indeed, no statement about prayer, experience, witnessing, the Holy Spirit, or the nature of Christ can even be understood without a reference to sound Bible doctrine.

The reason for this is clear: sound doctrine is that set of definitions without which nothing else can be understood. The preaching of Christ was doctrinal (Matthew 22:33; Mark 1:22; Luke 4:32). We are to obey from the heart that form of doctrine delivered unto us (Romans 6:17). We are to be conscious of offenses contrary to the doctrine of Christianity (Romans 16:17). We are to teach no other doctrine (1 Timothy 1:3). We are to give ourselves to sound doctrine (1 Timothy 1:10) and to good doctrine (1 Timothy 4:6). We are to concentrate on reading, exhortation, and doctrine (1 Timothy 4:13).

Scripture says further, "Take heed unto thyself, and unto the doctrine" (1 Timothy 4:16). "Let the elders that rule well be counted worthy of double honor, especially they who labor in the word and doctrine" (1 Timothy 5:17). "That the name of God and his doctrine be not blasphemed" (1 Timothy 6:1). "Exhort with all longsuffering and doctrine" (2 Timothy 4:2). "For the time will come when they will not endure sound doctrine" (2 Timothy 4:3). "Holding fast the faithful word as he hath been taught, that he may be able by sound doctrine both to exhort and to convince the gainsayers" (Titus 1:9). "Whoso-

ever transgresseth, and abideth not in the doctrine of
Christ, hath not God. He that abideth in the doctrine of
Christ, he hath both the Father and the Son" (2 John 9).

In the light of the clear teaching of Scripture, it is
frightening to hear a Christian speaker naively declare
that "what we need today is not more theology and doctrine but more experience!" Such assertions indicate a
shortage of biblical understanding. They are not only untrue—but dangerously untrue. They pave the way for satanic activity.

Sound doctrine is the basis or the understanding of
every other aspect of the Christian life. Without it, no
Christian can communicate with another. Indeed, without it, the Christian is made vulnerable to the subversion
of the doctrines of his infernal majesty, the devil.

An understanding of *sound* doctrine makes it possible for us to perceive *un*sound doctrine. The Bible contains a number of clear statements by the devil himself of
his doctrine, the false doctrines of the universe. From his
assertions, we can understand the doctrines that the devil
may use to subvert us. This kind of an understanding will
mean that we never again need be ignorant of his devices,
the most deadly of which is doctrinal subversion.

When Paul warns Timothy of the possibility of doctrinal subversion, he is not speaking of weird people who
represent the lunatic fringe of aberrant religion. The
stringy-haired fanatics or the sweaty emotionalizers are
not the object of Paul's concern here. He is warning reasonable, thoughtful, Christian people. He has in mind people of enough interest to study religious things. He is
referring to individuals with a general knowledge of the Bible. Some knowledge, at least, is necessary before one can
wrest the Scripture to his own destruction.

It follows, of course, that a general knowledge of the
Bible does little good. Who of us have not heard about people who are members or grand masters of some mystical
organization, that quote an obscure verse from Ecclesias-

tes and thereby make the claim that their views are Bible-based? Tragically, a high percentage of the individuals who attend our churches are woefully devoid of a knowledge of Scripture. Their knowledge is simply not sufficient to give them a reason for their faith or to equip them to defend the gospel. Alexander Pope's warning that "a little learning is a dangerous thing" applies not only to philosophy but even more emphatically to Christianity. The lunatic fringe of Christianity is well populated by people who picked up some verse of Scripture many years ago and have been attempting to live on it ever since.

We must know the details of Scripture, the whole of Scripture, and the doctrines of Scripture. No one who does not know the Scripture in detail can claim to know the Scripture at all.

When discussing the dangers of satanic doctrinal subversion, the Bible is clearly warning thoughtful people. Let no one say, "I don't claim to be a witch, a prophetess or a magician; therefore, I am not really vulnerable to satanic activity." Think again. The witches and the magicians provide Satan with some fun and games along the way, but his real activity is subverting the insiders, the reasonable, and the semi-studious with false doctrine.

To *believe* the wrong thing is far more serious than to *do* the wrong thing. Ask yourself: How many doctrines of the devil do I really understand? With how many have I already been subverted?

Doctrinal subversion is more deadly than witchcraft.

2

"God Is a Cosmic Sadist"

No person is infected by the disease of sin until he has first been led to believe the wrong thing. The tyranny and death that sin brings start when a person begins to believe a false view about God, himself, life, or divine purpose. The devil's doctrines are that ultimate set of false views that he constantly attempts to insinuate into the thinking of men. Far more than witchcraft or magic, Satan uses "almost true" intellectual propositions to appeal to reasonable people. His most effective work is done—not in saloons and brothels—but in the minds of men. He is a destroyer of truth. He is a liar from the beginning. He is a pusher—not merely of marijuana or heroin—but of false propositions. He promotes an addiction to lies.

Thankfully, the Bible makes a number of plain statements that quote the devil himself. We are able thereby to know the propositional falsehoods that Satan pushes. Contrasting these "doctrines" with sound biblical doctrine will equip us more than any other way to resist our hateful enemy.

The first doctrine that Satan categorically expresses in the Bible is found in the opening words of his conversation with Eve, the mother of the human race. With the voice of the serpent, he speaks to her, saying, "Yea, hath

God said, Ye shall not eat of every tree of the garden?"
Many hold that Satan is simply casting doubt on the truth
of the statements of God. He is certainly doing that, but he
is also operating on a deeper level than merely the production of doubt.

Satan is actually making the suggestion that would
amount to, "Isn't God really saying that you cannot eat of
any of the fruit of the Garden?" *The Living Bible* puts it
well, saying, "The serpent was the craftiest of all the creatures the Lord God had made. So the serpent came to the
woman. "Really?" he asked. "*None* of the fruit in the garden? God says you mustn't eat *any* of it?" (Genesis 3:1).

What a clever ploy! The enemy suggests that God is a
moral tyrant, so bluenosed that He has forbidden His creatures any enjoyment whatsoever. The implication is that
God filled the Garden with a delightful array of delicious
fruits to taunt man, forbidding him to eat of any of these
fruits. God is therefore a negativist who made man merely
to frustrate him. He is a cosmic sadist, inflicting an impossible set of rules and punishments upon man. God is
therefore impossible to please, a total tyrant, so the best
thing to do is to chuck the whole thing as of right now.

From her reaction, we see that Eve was ever so slightly attracted to this proposition, partially subverted by the
first lying suggestion of Satan. She responds by saying,
"We may eat of the fruit of the trees of the garden; but of
the fruit of the tree which is in the midst of the garden,
God hath said, Ye shall not eat it, neither shall ye touch it,
lest ye die."

To Eve's credit, she correctly recalls the words of God
concerning what fruit is to be eaten and what is not. God
has been essentially positive about this instruction. He
had said, "Of *every* tree of the garden thou mayest freely
eat; but of the tree of the knowledge of good and evil, thou
shalt not eat of it, for in the day that thou eatest thereof,
thou shalt surely die. Eve quoted God correctly as to His
permission to eat of the trees of the Garden.

But after this, she reaches a critical point and begins to slip. The beginning of her defection from truth follows when she misrepresents God as saying, "Neither shall ye touch it." This was not part of the original instructions. This statement by Eve represents a concession to the God-is-a-sadist suggestion of Satan. She has moved an inch in Lucifer's direction.

What is the truth of the matter concerning privilege and prohibition? The fact is that God had been almost totally permissive in His instructions. He noted the large number of trees and plants bearing delicious fruit that grew across the wide expanse of the Garden of Eden. There are hundreds of varieties of fruits known to man today. We may be sure that each of these and possibly more were represented in their most luscious form in Eden. About all of these and their enjoyments God had said a resounding "Yes, they are all yours; go ahead and eat them and enjoy them to the full."

Before Adam and Eve was the possibility of many delicious involvements in eating the fruit of the Garden. The instructions that God had given were—*with but one exception*—on the positive, permissive side. God had in effect said, "I'm for you! I made you with palates to enjoy the exquisite sweetness of the strawberry and the grape. The tart delight of the crab apple, the bananas, oranges, pears—they all are yours." Every physical gratification was given to the couple in the Garden. Every pleasure, every fulfillment was theirs.

Concerning only one tree in the Garden God had said, "But of the tree of the knowledge of good and evil, thou shalt not eat of it, for in the day that thou eatest thereof, thou shalt surely die." It is clear that *almost* everything in the environment of Adam and Eve was covered by God's permission, even His encouragement. One prohibition as against hundreds of permissions is approximately the moral formula of Eden. There was only one way in which Adam and Eve could sin; that, of course, was in eating the forbidden fruit. On everything else all systems were go.

Satan's trick was to reverse all of this and turn the permissions of God into prohibitions. "Everything is a no-no," Satan is implying. "God doesn't love you; He hates you and toys with you. He gave you an appetite so He could starve you. He gave you life only that He may better enjoy your death." Satan, his own mind already distorted with the workings of sin, successfully stamped this perverted view of God into the thinking of Eve.

An understanding of this doctrine (that God is a prohibitionist) is most useful information in the situation in which we find ourselves. Is Satan still pushing this doctrine? Indeed he is.

In our time, both the world and the church seem to have conspired to present the gracious Creator of the universe as a tyrant. The image that many have of Him is that of a despot in heaven looking down at people having fun, quickly moving to break up the game. Believing this satanic distortion, modern Adams and Eves quickly turn from grateful appreciation of their wide privileges to a fatal resentment of the few things that are forbidden to them.

For instance, I have often talked with a college student and listened to the philosophy that he has developed under the influence of his educational environment. He has opportunities most young people have never known. His university has millions of dollars in buildings and equipment, libraries full of books, air-conditioned classrooms, and knowledgeable professors who pass on their wisdom and experience to him. His education is funded by the taxes and contributions that come from thousands of people whom he will never see. As a result, he is given leisure time and educational resources from which, if he chose, he could become a worthy scholar. God and society are saying yes in a thousand ways to him. "Go! Do! Be! Expand your mind! Increase the breadth of your vision and ability. The world is yours; go and take it!" Society is pouring privileges upon this student almost beyond measure.

Then I have sadly noted that a new voice is heard within this young mind. It whispers like it has done before, "You're nothing but a patsy. Privilege? Ha! This is a trick to make you a pawn of the establishment. God doesn't love you; He hates you, and so does society. All of these 'gifts' and 'opportunities' are the crumbs that fall from the table of the rich. You are the object of a vicious conspiracy. You are a fool to believe that anyone gets so much for so little." With frightening predictability, our young student believes this. The devil has subverted him. He listens with keener interest to the voice that says, "So look, revolution is the way to go. Smash the establishment! Liberate! The way to build is to destroy! Ashes are the steps to the future."

So the author of all evil, whose own heart is filled with violence, seduces legions to follow him. With neat finesse, he is often able to introduce drugs, illicit sex, and even violent crime as "authentic moral symbols of that righteous rebellion." Only too much later does Satan's hapless victim realize, as he stands amid the wreckage of his life, that he has been duped by the devil. He has been consumed by the fire that he started when he began to listen to the whispered suggestions of the evil one.

Rejecting a hundred permitted things and reaching for one forbidden thing is a common characteristic of the human race from earliest childhood through all of life. How many a loving family circle has been blasted apart because of a foolish father who was tricked by the devil into a mistaken attitude about the delights and privileges available to him. With Satan's help, he fantasizes that the lust of a moment can somehow be better than these. He believes the devil's doctrine that God is a moral tyrant whose law "deserves" to be broken. So the devil makes a fool of him.

Even the little child experiences Satan's doctrine. Forbidden to reach into the flame of a candle but given a dozen toys to play with, his furtive glance turns from his toys, and he looks with desire at the beckoning flame. In some simple but perverse way, he believes that the candle flame is a joy that he really deserves. His parents have said yes to a hundred things and no to one. And all of these present toys are inferior to that. When his parent's back is turned, he reaches for the flickering flame. The results are sharp and immediate.

The searing results of sin are not usually so painful and immediate. The normal results of most kinds of sin in our present world are progressive in time and achieve their final fatality in eternity. "Sin, when it is finished, bringeth forth death" (James 1:15). It is true that the wages of sin is death, but God in His mercy often delays the final payoff in order to give us time to repent. This temporary period of reflection that is given to us by the grace of God, following an act of sin, is misinterpreted by some. They argue from the lack of apparent consequences of a given sin that nothing really happened and, therefore, the prohibitions of God were not really that serious. Under this foolish line of logic, many have interpreted the patience of God as inefficiency, weakness, or inattention on His part. As against this, we have the clear warning of Scripture, "My spirit shall not always strive with man" (Genesis 6:3).

Nevertheless, despite every evidence of the grace of God, man again and again feels rising within him the sense that all is forbidden and everything is sin, therefore what's the use! His attitude amounts to the familiar bromide, "Everything I enjoy is either illegal, immoral, or fattening."

When man starts to think negatively about God, he finds himself in the beginning of his real trouble. In his bitterness, he no longer feels God's warm sunshine or His gentle rain. The beauty and blessedness of all that is permitted to him gradually turns to the ashes of resentment. He becomes a total cynic. He feels it is a ridiculous proposition to suggest that the best things in life are free.

But it is still true; the best things in life *are* free. Take another look! Is it not true that each of us is surrounded with a thousand potential fulfillments that we could miss because of a sick preoccupation with a single fascinating garbage heap? How long since we rejoiced in the budding newness of springtime? What pornographic movie can compare to three nights of Kansas sunsets? What stick of marijuana can bring a natural high like jogging in the surf? What floor show in Las Vegas can produce a turn-on comparable to a single reading of C. S. Lewis's *Four Loves*?

The things freely given to us by God are infinitely greater than the necessary and protective prohibitions of life. The problem is that Satan inflames our resentment about how wrong it is for God to say, "Thou shalt not commit adultery," or, "Thou shalt not steal," or "Thou shalt not kill." These simple prohibitions are obviously made for our own good.

Every parent has been accused, "You never let me do *anything*!" when he was imposed upon by what he considered a minor prohibition. Satan wants us to accuse God of the same thing.

In this first doctrine, then, Satan promotes a lie. He changes a specific law to a general prohibition. Any person who believes that God is a tyrant and that He is against us has been subverted by this first satanic doctrine. Notice the contrast in the promise of the Bible, "Delight thyself also in the Lord; and he shall give thee the desires of thine heart" (Psalm 37:4). "No good thing will he withhold from them that walk uprightly" (Psalm 84:11). "If God be for us, who can be against us? He that spared not his own Son, but delivered him up for us all, how shall he not with him also freely give us all things?" (Romans 8:31-32). "All things are lawful unto me," says

Paul, "but all things are not expedient" (1 Corinthians 6:12). God is the God of permission, not prohibition. The Scripture says that God "giveth us richly all things to enjoy" (1 Timothy 6:17). God says yes one hundred times for every one time that He says no. Even when He says no, He still allows us to disobey Him, providing of course, we are willing to pay the consequences, which is also an evidence of His grace.

Notice, however, by the nature of these promises, that there has been a subtle change in the order of things since the days of Adam and Eve. When they sinned, they brought into the world a spiritual infection, a moral imbalance that makes it necessary for us to sound a warning about the nature of permission and prohibition in our time. While it was possible for Eve to sin in only one way, it is possible for us to sin in a thousand ways. Therefore, by infecting the world with sin, his infernal majesty has almost brought to pass what he suggested to Eve as being true. In contrast to the Garden of Eden, it is true in our present age that almost everything is indeed wrong. Even "the plowing of the wicked is sin" (Proverbs 21:4). "The sacrifice of the wicked is an abomination to the Lord" (Proverbs 15:8). All those things that are not of faith are sin (Romans 14:23). We who are the heirs to Adam and Eve are under the nearly total prohibition of God, and we do not move from prohibition to permission until we disavow the kingdom of darkness and move into the kingdom of light. We must go back to innocence before the first permissions of God can apply in our lives.

The only way then for us to reenter that state of spiritual innocence is by receiving Jesus Christ as Savior. The call from the slavery of sin into the freedom for which we were created is implicit in the invitation of Christ, "Come unto me, all ye that labour and are heavy laden, and I will give you rest" (Matthew 11:28). "Him that cometh to me I will in no wise cast out" (John 6:37). God makes clear the utter necessity of receiving His grace and permission by receiving Christ. "He that hath the Son hath life; and he that hath not the Son of God hath not life" (1 John 5:12). "He that believeth on the Son hath everlasting life: and he that believeth not the Son shall not see life; but the wrath of God abideth on him" (John 3:36). "He that believeth on him is not condemned: but he that believeth not is condemned already, because he hath not believed in the name of the only begotten Son of God" (John 3:18).

When our parents sinned, they moved all of humanity into the horrible slave market of sin. In this slave market, we were born; in it, we live; and in it, we die, unless we are purchased from these sinful environs. When we receive Christ, we are set free from the bondage of sin, and we move from total prohibition to wide permission under the umbrella of the grace of God. Obviously, only the Christian can see God as He really is, a gracious and loving personal Being!

Satan is a liar when he continues to insist that God is a tyrant and all is prohibited. There are a few people who know and can prove that this satanic doctrine is a lie. These few are growing in number every day. They are called Christians.

3

"God
Is a
Liar"

Most rebellions begin with the corrosive emotion of resentment.

While talking to Eve in the garden, Satan had successfully introduced the proposition that God is a moralist so severe that He simply cannot be pleased. This produced resentment in Eve, laying the groundwork for a new attitude in her life, affecting her relationship with her heavenly Father. This new attitude is mistrust. Because of Eve's response to his first doctrine, he boldly moves from a question to an assertion. Satan is now quite dogmatic: "You shall not surely die." Here is revealed the second doctrine of the devil, namely, "God is a liar; He cannot be trusted, and His Word is not true."

Satan is emboldened to make this evil assertion because of Eve's exaggeration of the divine prohibition. Eve indeed attempted to repel the satanic thrust that everything is evil by saying, "We may indeed eat of the fruit of the trees of the Garden." At this point, however, she shows that she has already been partly subverted by Satan's statement, in that she states a revised version of God's warning concerning the tree with the forbidden fruit. She says, "But of the fruit of the tree which is in the midst of the garden, God hath said, Ye shall not eat of it, *neither shall ye touch it*, lest ye die" (emphasis added). The fact is that God had made no such prohibition. His rule was simply that the fruit of the tree must not be *eaten*. He had said nothing about *touching* the tree. Here, Eve is beginning to rationalize, setting up a false basis on which she may later blame God, complaining that His laws are too stringent and therefore impossible to keep. Satan quickly detects this rationalization and moves ahead aggressively in his plan. He now declares, "That's a lie; you shall not surely die."

In making this statement, Satan gives us two useful clues about himself. The first illustrates the nature of his activities; the second reveals another point of his doctrine.

As to the nature of his activities, we can now discern the fact that Satan moves in the lives of people from a lesser degree to the greater. He begins his assault by establishing a small beachhead and moves from this point of moral fault into a program of larger conquest. He ultimately intends to consume us, but this devouring begins with the smallest nibble. He conceals his objectives, making it appear that he is devoted to our happiness. Behind this smoke screen of hypocritical compassion, he veils his true intentions. He promises freedom from death but in fact is a murderer from the beginning. He has no compassion whatsoever!

Satan still uses the same technique of entrapping his victim little by little, until the person is committed to him. No one was ever lured into alcoholism by having presented to him the picture of a hopeless drunk draped over a mailbox or retching in the gutter. The working of Satan is usually initiated in the smallest things, like social drinking, and only later develops into the yawning chasm of despair that sin invariably produces.

The initial attractiveness of sin does not prefigure its consequences. That makes it most difficult to warn sin's novice adequately of the hideous thing he will finally make of himself.

Now, having established his beachhead of doubt, Satan moves to consolidate his position, expanding from doubt to denial. "Thou shalt not surely die." In this, we see the second doctrine of Satan. God is a liar. His word is not true. Satan again affirms that another system of truth takes precedence over the word of God. Here is the first appearance of an alternative epistemology. Truth has been newly defined. Satan has postulated another authority more final, more "true" than the very Word of the living God. So began the first problem of the universe, the problem of truth. Ever since this first lie, the world has repeatedly asked the question, What is truth?

Satan's answer to this question is that truth is anything except the word of God. Consistent with this false doctrine, he continues to confuse the issue of final authority in many ways in our present world. He works to get people to believe any one of his many alternatives to truth. He would have us accept the proposition that truth is ever changing (relativism), or purely personal (subjectivism), or only what we can see (empiricism), or encounter experiences (existentialism), or purely syllogistic (rationalism), or completely abstract (platonic idealism), or events (phenomenalism), or synonymous with creation (pantheism), or a blend of the seen and the unseen (psycho-physical monism), or workability (pragmatism), or a hundred similarly false alternatives. The history of thought is the account of efforts by successive generations of thinkers to re-answer the vital question, What is truth?

Since Satan introduced it, the problem of truth and error has made impossible the solution of any other problem that confronts the human scene. Every difficulty that has ever beset men has come because of an inadequate answer to the question, What is truth?

What *is* truth?

Purely human rationality cannot answer that question, for all answers that involve the use of reason must begin with a premise that is not based on reason. We must turn to another source, and there is only one other source.

That other source is *revelation*. The reason for this should also be quite obvious. Being finite beings, we have no way of discovering ultimate truth unless that thing, or force, or *person* chooses to reveal himself to us. Being finite beings, we must depend on revelation for the knowledge of ultimate things. Do we have such a revelation of final truth? Yes. That final truth is the Bible, the living Word of God. The Bible claims the unique distinction of being the Word of God. The phrase "thus saith the Lord" or its equivalent occurs over two thousand times in the Old Testament. Isaiah said, "Moreover the Lord said unto me. . . . For the Lord spake thus to me" (Isaiah 8:1, 11). David claimed, "The Spirit of the Lord spake by me, and his word was in my tongue. The God of Israel said, The Rock of Israel spake to me" (2 Samuel 23:1-3). Jeremiah asserted, "Then the Lord put forth his hand, and touched my mouth. And the Lord said unto me, Behold, I have put my words in thy mouth" (Jeremiah 1:9; cf. 5:14; 7:27; 13:12).

The New Testament writers make the same claim about the inspiration of the Old Testament, asserting that the prophets spoke the Word of God. "God, who at sundry times and in divers manners spake in time past unto the fathers by the prophets" (Hebrews 1:1). Old Testament prophecies concerning Jesus Christ were considered to be what the Lord had spoken by the prophet (see Matthew 1:22; 2:15). Luke claimed that the Holy Spirit spoke "by the mouth of David" (Acts 1:16) and also to your fathers through Isaiah the prophet (Acts 28:25). The Jews of Jesus' day believed that the Old Testament was the infallible Word of God, accepting in every detail the testimony of its writers that what they said was what God said.

We also have the testimony of Jesus Christ as to the inspiration and infallibility of the Word of God. In Matthew 5:18 He says, "Till heaven and earth pass, one jot or one tittle shall in no way pass from the law, till all be fulfilled" (NSRB). This passage makes clear how highly Jesus regarded the Old Testament.

Christ, in many ways, restated the infallibility of the Old Testament Scripture. In Mark 7:13 He says, "Thus invalidating the word of God by your tradition which you have handed down" (NASB); in Luke 16:31, "If they hear not Moses and the prophets, neither will they be persuaded, though one rose from the dead." In Luke 24:27 He says, "And beginning with Moses and with all the prophets, He explained to them the things concerning Himself" (NASB); in John 10:35, "The scripture cannot be broken."

Looking forward to the revelation of God being progressively revealed in the exact words of the New Testament, Jesus said, "But the Helper, the Holy Spirit, whom the Father will send in My name, He will teach you all things, and bring to your remembrance all that I said to you" (John 14:26, NASB).

Add to this the testimony of the apostle Paul who wrote at least thirteen of the twenty-seven New Testament books. He wrote to Timothy, "All scripture is given by inspiration of God, and is profitable for doctrine, for reproof, for correction, for instruction in righteousness: that the man of God may be perfect, thoroughly furnished unto all good works" (2 Timothy 3:16-17). The word *inspiration* is the Greek word *theopneustos*, which is a compound of *theos* (God) and *neustos* (breathed).

In another place, Paul explains how revelation took place with him and with other writers of Scripture. In 1 Corinthians 2:12-13 he says, "Now we have received, not the spirit of the world, but the Spirit who is from God, that we might know the things freely given to us by God, which things we also speak, not in words taught by human wisdom, but in those taught by the Spirit, combining spiritual thoughts with spiritual words" (NASB).

The possession of this faithful Word from God gave Paul his claim to authority. He said, "If anyone thinks he is a prophet or spiritual, let him recognize that the things which I write to you are the Lord's commandment" (1 Corinthians 14:37, NASB).

Peter adds to our understanding of divine revelation by saying, "We have also a more sure word of prophecy, unto which ye do well to take heed, as unto a light that shineth in a dark place, until the day dawn, and the day star arise in your hearts; Knowing this first, that no prophecy of the scripture is of any private interpretation. For the prophecy came not at any time by the will of man, but holy men of God spoke as they were moved by the Holy Spirit (2 Peter 1:19-21, NSRB). Because of inspiration, Peter is able to write, "For all flesh is as grass, and all the glory of man as the flower of grass. The grass withereth, and the flower thereof falleth away; But the word of the Lord endureth for ever. And this is the word which by the gospel is preached unto you" (1 Peter 1:24-25).

The Christian's faith that the Bible is the very Word of the living God is utterly confirmed by every proven fact of learning that comes from outside the pages of Scripture. The findings of science, archaeology, psychology, history, chemistry, physics, and all other areas of inquiry, in discoveries that bear a relationship to the teaching of the Word of God, confirm without exception Scripture's claim to inspiration.

Truth produces results in lives. Millions of individuals call themselves Christians, claiming that their lives were transformed when they accepted the testimony of the Word of God at face value and received its offered Savior as their personal Deliverer from sin. This is the subjective argument, but it is an unshakable source of biblical confirmation within the lives of those who have received the Bible as the Word of God and believed in Jesus Christ.

The existence of this mass of unimpeachable data,

called the Bible, infuriates his infernal majesty, the devil. This is the reason that, as he said to Eve, he now says to this world in a thousand ways, "God's Word is not true; don't believe Him; believe *me*." Our generation, perhaps more than most, has seen the activity of Satan as he attempts to promote his second cardinal doctrine in many impressive ways. The person who would believe the Bible is pressed upon by many subversive voices that would beguile him into accepting some foundation for truth other than Scripture. Indeed, the Bible itself has been attacked in this century such as never before.

That attack began in the last century with Julius Wellhausen, one of the men who rules the world from his grave. In the late 1800s, German rationalism gave to the world the Graf-Wellhausen theory of Scripture. Wellhausen advanced the view that the Old Testament should be looked upon, not as the Word of God, but as an eloquent collection of documents written by capable scribes who gave their impressions about God, their witness to revelation.

This was the first modern attempt to place human reason, the ability of the human mind to analyze things, above the inspiration of the words of Scripture. This great attack of reason upon revelation became more and more successful as "thinking" people decided to pay themselves the compliment of being the judge of what the Bible teaches. Properly understood, the Bible judges us far more than we judge it.

German rationalism, with its higher critical view of Scripture, broke upon the Western world around the turn of the century. These sub-Christian ideas carried everything before them and created within Christianity a new phenomenon called liberalism. One after another, the major denominations of that day were subverted by the higher critical point of view, leaving the view that the Bible is the inspired Word of God and giving the right of critical judgment to the reason of men. For them, reason superseded revelation, and the Word of God could no longer be trusted.

Looking back now, we can see the catastrophic results of the denial of the truth of Scripture in the early part of this century. The liberals' slogan "Every day in every way, I am getting better and better" has been destroyed by two major wars in which millions have been killed. Wars, depressions, crime, and every form of evil continues to grow in our society. All of this gives the lie to the liberal suggestion that social action can fundamentally improve the course of mankind. The progressive degeneration of liberal theology finally produced the most obscene announcement in the history of the world, the absurd news that God is dead.

The latest version of pseudo-Christianity is Liberation Theology. Here God is contextualized into the social structure and is seen as identifying Himself with the poor and oppressed. The result is a Christian-Marxist hybrid that some say bridges the gap between Christianity and Marxism. In Liberation Theology the message of Christianity promises economic instead of spiritual liberation. Christ becomes a social revolutionary instead of a Savior.

Corrupt theology has also produced a corrupt "new morality." This religious establishment has produced the most godless concepts and anti-Christian philosophies imaginable to man. Church groups are now declaring that trial marriage is a legitimate involvement. (The Bible says, "Thou shalt not commit adultery," Exodus 20:14.) They have assured us that homosexuality is a legitimate expression of feeling. (The Scripture says, "They who commit such things are worthy of death," Romans 1:32.) They have published some of the most filthy pornography imaginable. (The Scripture says about the things that are done of them in secret, "Let it not be once named among you, as becometh saints," Ephesians 5:3.) They have advocated revolution against government. (The Bible says, "The powers that be are ordained of God," Romans 13:1.)

The list seems endless of the false points of view taken by some factions of our present religious establishment. When one rejects the final authority of the Word of God, he begins a process of corruption whereby his whole thought structure becomes a vast delusion.

Virtually all of the problems of our present age have come because we have turned from the truth of revelation to the sinking sand of mere human philosophy. Every psychiatric clinic, every automobile accident, and every graveyard testify to us that human reason is neither infallible nor eternal. Despite the obvious untrustworthiness of human reason, Satan still continues successfully to advance his argument that it is possible to place final trust in something else beside the Word of God. We must turn from the voice of Satan to the careful study of the Bible. A knowledge of the Bible is our best protection against the wiles of the devil. We do well to establish early in our lives the conviction that the Word of God, as against *any* alternative voice, will be our final authority. In making the decisions of life, we will never find the correct course unless we are willing to establish that course on the basis of the final authority of Scripture. We never will be able to establish a moral base for our lives and for our children unless that final reason for the moral course that we take is, "The Bible says so." Why is it wrong to steal? Because the Bible says, "Thou shalt not steal." Why is it wrong to commit adultery? Because the Bible says so. Why should children obey their parents? Because the Bible says so. Why should we worship God only? Because the Bible says so. Since God knows what is best for us, if He tells us in His Word not to do something, we had better believe it must be wrong for us.

Our old enemy, the devil, can twist any other human argument into a new basis for his hellish corruption. We must not allow him to twist the Word of God or cause us to believe that Scripture is no longer a solid foundation on which to build our lives. Any person who follows the lead-ing of anything apart from the clear and final truth of the Word of God is believing and committing himself to the devil's doctrine. He is rejecting the true doctrine of Jesus Christ. We will surely then sin against God unless we are protected by both a knowledge of and a commitment to the truth of the Scripture.

One of the additional implications of this doctrine of the devil is that there are no adverse consequences to disobedience to God. Here he is rewriting the Bible to read, "Whatsoever a man soweth, that shall he *not* also reap." God said, "The way of the transgressor is hard" (Proverbs 13:15), but Satan would have us to believe that sin is fun. God's Word warns, "The wages of sin is death," but Satan is still at work pushing the opposite point of view. Modern thought would still have us believe that the path of sin will produce fun, happiness, fulfillment, and worthwhile achievement in life. We are never told about the suicides, diseases, and agonizing deaths of people who have believed Satan's philosophy. Every person who rejects the Bible and attempts to live without Christ is a fool, subverted by the second doctrine of his infernal majesty.

4

"There Is
No
Destiny"

"**N**ow Eve, let's face it. You are so small and God is so big that there's no way you will ever be anything more than a pathetic little pygmy in His sight. He obviously made you in this limited fashion because He wants some little automatons who will always do His bidding. You and Adam will never be more than God's little slaves.

"It's time to strike out on your own, Eve, the name of the game is *autonomy*.

"Eve, God knows that if you eat of this fruit, you will be like a god. That is why He told you not to eat it. I promise you, Eve, that God never will bring you anywhere near His level, and so you had better take matters into your own hands. Assert yourself! Take a bite of this fruit. Not only will you not die, but you will be like a god. You will know what it's all about by *your own* experience and knowledge! It will put you on a level with *Him*. Take some, and give some to Adam to eat, and you are on the road to destiny. We can make a plan for your life, Eve, that will make God's little diagram look like peanuts."

So it was that the serpent revealed the third satanic doctrine: there is no destiny. "For God doth know that in the day ye eat thereof, then your eyes shall be opened, and ye shall be as gods, knowing good and evil" (Genesis

3:5). With this statement, Satan comes to the daring conclusion of his conversation with Eve. He has already pressed upon Eve the lie that God is a tyrant and His word is not to be trusted. He now suggests that God made man to be His slave forever. Establishing this, Satan can suggest that Eve take matters into her own hands. He convinces her that she must take a shortcut to personal realization.

The question of divine destiny is an important one for Satan. He has made it a point of his doctrine to deny this. Is there a mighty purpose for which we were created? What really was the purpose for which God made man in His image?

We are told in the Bible that God created man in order to make him ultimately higher than the angels and put the world to come in subjection under him (Hebrews 2:8). God has an eternal plan for each of our lives, and He works to bring that exciting plan to fulfillment. We are indeed people of destiny! The Bible is filled with promises of a most glorious eternity, a fabulous future that God has provided for man. The imagination of every human mind should be quickened by these promises of God:

> Thou wilt shew me the path of life: in thy presence is fulness of joy; at thy right hand there are pleasures for evermore. (Psalm 16:11)

> Eye hath not seen, nor ear heard, neither have entered into the heart of man, the things which God hath prepared for them that love him. (1 Corinthians 2:9)

> For unto the angels hath he not put in subjection the world to come, whereof we speak. But one in a certain place testified, saying, What is man, that thou art mindful of him? or the son of man, that thou visitest him? (Hebrews 2:5-6)

> And he shewed me a pure river of water of life, clear as crystal, proceeding out of the throne of God and of the

Lamb. In the midst of the street of it, and on either side of the river, was there the tree of life, which bare twelve manner of fruits, and yielded her fruit every month: and the leaves of the tree were for the healing of the nations. And there shall be no more curse: but the throne of God and of the Lamb shall be in it; and his servants shall serve him: And they shall see his face; and his name shall be in their foreheads. And there shall be no night there; and they need no candle, neither light of the sun; for the Lord God giveth them light: and they shall reign for ever and ever. (Revelation 22:1-5)

The Bible teaches a most exalted purpose for which God created man. This purpose is to become like God Himself, to partake in His uncreated and eternal life, and to share with Him the rulership of the universe.

Sin entered the world because Satan was able to cause Eve to forget temporarily the doctrine of divine destiny. She temporarily believed the antitruth that God had no purpose for her life. Satan's argument was astonishingly successful with Eve. "And when the woman saw that the tree was good for food, and that it was pleasant to the eyes, and a tree to be desired to make one wise, she took of the fruit thereof, and did eat, and gave also unto her husband with her; and he did eat" (Genesis 3:6). With this decision, Eve traded the bright promise of eternal life for the instant but temporary fulfillment of the lust of the flesh. The proximity of the things that she could see and feel became larger in that moment than the "abstractions" of a yet unrealized future.

Having succeeded in such fine fashion with Eve, Satan, we may be sure, will continue to push his argument that divine destiny is a nonexistent abstraction, while reality is the immediate circle of fulfillments available in this present moment.

What is the true comparative value between this life and the life to come? The Christian understands this value differential. Paul explains it well: "For our light affliction, which is but for a moment, worketh for us a far more exceeding and eternal weight of glory; while we look not at the things which are seen, but at the things which are not seen: for the things which are seen are temporal; but the things which are not seen are eternal" (2 Corinthians 4:17-18). This affirmation stands in sure contrast to satanic doctrine and to the spirit of our present age.

In our time, the here and now is invariably presented as infinitely more important than the yet to come. One is thought a fool to deny himself the immediate fulfillments of this present moment in favor of some better but future realization. To do a thing for moral reasons rather than for immediate gratification is thought laughable by the present conventional wisdom. "Do it now! Live now!" is the rallying cry of this day and hour. The gospel that presents a hope for eternity sounds like a pleasant but impractical abstraction to the deaf ears of our now-oriented generation.

This spirit of "now" as against "then" has had influence, even in the ranks of the church. Recently, I was in a meeting where the congregation sang,

> There's a land that is fairer than day,
> And by faith we can see it afar;
> Where the Father waits over the way
> To prepare us a dwelling place there.
>
> In the sweet by and by
> We shall meet on that beautiful shore.
> In the sweet by and by,
> We shall meet on that beautiful shore.

It occurred to me, as we sang this blessed old Christian hymn, that it had been a long time since I had even heard it sung. I realized then that much of our music, teaching, and preaching has to do with the relevance of Christianity to this present moment. We hear a lot about involvement in society, keeping up with our changing times, being sensitive to political, racial, and social problems, and a host of other contemporary themes.

The social gospel was hardly the emphasis of the writers of the New Testament. Paul sums up all of the affairs, joys, delights, and involvements of this lifetime with a few short words: "For our light affliction, which is but for a moment." The teaching of the New Testament is that we have a short sojourn through this world. In it, we are to understand Christian doctrine, communicate it to others in the brief time that we have, and then step into the presence of our heavenly Father. The New Testament scarcely mentions relevance and social involvement as it is currently being emphasized in Christian writing and preaching.

In the first chapter of Romans, God announces three times that He has given this world up! He has turned it over to uncleanness, to vile affections, and to a reprobate mind. The epistles following Romans present a hitherto unmentioned message—that the church is the body of Christ and is already seated in the heavenlies with Him. The New Testament speaks little of permanent human associations or cultural involvement and social relevance, but talks of being pilgrims and strangers in a condemned and unsavable society. It concedes incidentally that we should "do good unto all men," but gives more importance to our helping others of "the household of faith" (Galatians 6:10). The emphasis is upon preparing for eternal life rather than those activities that are for this life alone.

What has happened to this message of eternal destiny? How often have we reminded ourselves that "if in this life only we have hope in Christ, we are of all men most miserable" (1 Corinthians 15:19)? The grand themes of the New Testament are our future resurrection, the second coming of Christ, the judgment of God upon this world, and the necessity of snatching souls from this world's entrapments "like brands from the burning." Eve rejected the message of eternal destiny in exchange for present knowledge, satisfaction, and fulfillment. Is it possible that even organized Christianity is moving now in this direction?

We now hear of a new view in the church, which might be called "presentism." It states that Christians have a mandate to dominate, rule, and master this present world. (The Bible calls it "this present evil world," Galatians 1:4.) Beware of this pathway declaring that the church is given human dominion in this day of grace. The followers of such a view claim that "the kingdom is now!" Is it?

But the most important application of this satanic doctrine is to our personal lives. Each person who believes more in the fulfillments of the present than in the eternal purpose of God in his life has been subverted by this third satanic doctrine.

Another implication of the devil's third doctrine that can become a valuable lesson to each of us is the suggestion that experience is always the best teacher. The expression "knowing good and evil" refers to knowing by experience. He is saying to Eve that she will know by experience good and evil; she will become as God.

Nothing is further from the truth than to suggest that experience is the best teacher in things with moral implications. The person who is steeped in sin knows little about either sin or righteousness. It is the person who stands against the current who knows the strength of a river rather than the one who drifts downstream with the water. The person who is asleep comprehends neither sleep nor wakefulness.

Nevertheless, Satan is able to subvert relatively moral people on the basis of the argument. "Do it; only then will you understand it." Many a moral rationalist has fallen into the addiction of sin under the argument that by doing it, he will be better able to understand and help those in the same mess. He believed the satanic suggestion that experience is the best teacher.

Actually, experience in sin so dulls the senses as to make understanding of anything impossible. The indulgence in any vice from gluttony to illicit sex soon produces a deadness of feeling and comprehension so that even the indulgence itself becomes boring. So it is that all of our lusts, after their initial fulfillment, progressively starve us. Experience in immorality teaches us nothing. It merely increases a debt that we are made progressively more incapable of paying with each repeated experience. The advice "Don't knock it till you've tried it" is a lie that originated with Satan.

A further implication that can also add to our moral understanding is that there is a valid shortcut to fulfillment, to destiny. The implied promise of eating the forbidden fruit was that Eve would become *instantly* wise, mature, Godlike, and self-realized. There are few greater lies that Satan is able to pass into naive hearts than the lie that there is a shortcut to maturity or destiny.

Sadly, that lie is being preached today. Millions of promoters, from their own soapboxes, are saying, "Here is the simple, fulfilling answer. Do this one thing and you will have it all." Many people believe that alcohol, drugs, sex, and money are the keys to self-realization.

And those promising easy answers are not always outside of the religious establishment. Within the church, there is often the suggestion that some experience, some thrilling phenomenon, will produce instant maturity and a total relationship with God. One often hears the implied promise that one great ecstasy or one instant spiritual formula will produce a miraculous, divine enlightenment that is available in no other way. Unsuspecting Christians are following these implied promises as never before.

The truth is, there is no shortcut to knowledge, maturity, or destiny. All of these spiritual panaceas are in succession to the satanic doctrine that in effect says, "Do this one thing and you will have it all." The Bible gives us an entirely different picture. When we receive Jesus

Christ as our Savior, we are blessed with all spiritual blessings in heavenly places in Christ. But the road from innocence to maturity is long and difficult. Daily we are to be involved in the program of "perfecting holiness in the fear of God" (2 Corinthians 7:1). The process of maturing that prepares us for our eternal and heavenly responsibilities involves suffering, rejection, persecution, complex moral decisions, study, prayer, tireless labor, successes, failures, and the chastening of God. No message is more cruel to preach to the new Christian than the idea that there is an instant, giant step to maturity that comes through some unique involvement or experience.

Even evangelical Christianity is infected with the notion that there is a special, sinless life that comes as a result of a mysterious, spiritual step that produces an immense, one-time gain in our lives. The Christian faith itself is not unaffected by the influence of sub-Christian doctrines, and we are living in an age in which this effect continues to grow. The doctrine of instant maturity is one of them.

Paul believed no such delusion. Speaking of his own situation, he says, "Not as though I had already attained, either were already perfect [mature]: but I follow after, if that I may apprehend that for which also I am apprehended of Christ Jesus (Philippians 3:12). Christian sanctification comes to us in a *positional* sense instantly and totally when we receive Christ. *Progressive* sanctification is a daily and laborious task and will not and cannot be fulfilled so long as we live in a sinful world.

That is indeed the way God has ordained it. Earth is like a university, and our course of study will never be complete so long as we live on this campus. The moment a person believes that he has achieved an exalted plane in life, at that moment, the evil one has successfully cut off the educational process that alone can perfect real holiness in life. How many millions of Christians have been fixed in a state of tragic immaturity because they have believed a doctrine of instant perfection that has no basis in Scripture? Spiritual infants populate our churches and become problems because they have not continued to grow in grace and in the knowledge of our Lord and Savior, Jesus Christ.

Finally, the doctrine that the pursuit of God is a pointless errand has been the great inhibition to Christian evangelism. Of those who neglect or refuse to receive Christ as their Savior, the largest portion do so because they believe that the way to fulfillment is along another road. They pursue business acheivements, personal pleasure, prestige, or other forms of human accomplishment as the path to success as they perceive it. Each individual who is not a Christian believes that there is a more valuable course to follow in life than the spiritual one.

Millions in their spiritual blindness believe the satanic doctrine that there is another path to destiny beside receiving Christ as Savior and growing in the Christian life. Satan makes the world appear to present great promise, but once again, this is a promise that cannot be fulfilled. He promises, but he does not perform.

Despite this lack of performance, people continue to believe that the path to destiny is in some other direction beside God. Deciding against the will of God for their lives, they move into wasted years and a lost eternity.

They discover too late that the only purpose worth pursuing was the exciting plan that God has for their life. To believe any other point of view is to be subverted by a satanic doctrine.

5

"God Is Not Worthy"

Revolution is always built on ideology. Give people something to believe, and they will join your cause.

The roar of cannons is the final outgrowth of a doctrine that produces new convictions, motivating the participants to revolution. Revolutions would never come to pass if there were not revolutionary ideas first. Each revolution in history began with propagandists promoting a concept with which they motivated others.

The point is that ideas have consequences. External activities come to pass because of concepts or convictions, held in the heart, which motivate the will and produce actions. When the Hitlers, Mussolinis, and Jim Joneses of the world want to activate people, they must first ideologize them. They first tell them not what to do, but what to believe. If they can cause a false view of life to take root within a heart, dangerous and destructive actions can be carried out by otherwise normal people. False ideas, when acted upon, produce ruinous results.

The cry of "Down with the establishment!" may sound like just so many words. Those words, however, if translated into action, could become hard realities of terror, assassination, and death. There are people preaching revolution today who, if their words are to be taken at face

value, are really advocating the murder of millions. Their
plans, if allowed to become actions, would turn a nation
into a cemetery.

Satan has the same intention; he would like to turn
the whole world into a cemetery. If the fourth point in Satan's doctrinal structure were believed and practiced by
all the nations, we would see exactly that result. Indeed,
the Bible teaches that there is coming a time when all the
world will rebel against God. Satan's doctrine? God is not
worthy to rule the universe. Revolution then is appropriate for Satan. Scripture says,

> Why do the heathen rage, and the people imagine a vain
> thing? The kings of the earth set themselves, and the
> rulers take counsel together, against the Lord, and
> against his anointed, saying, Let us break their bands
> asunder, and cast away their cords from us. He that sit-
> teth in the heavens shall laugh: the Lord shall have
> them in derision. Then shall he speak unto them in his
> wrath, and vex them in his sore displeasure. (Psalm 2:1-
> 5)

This describes that final world rebellion that will cul-
minate in the most devastating battle in history, Armaged-
don. By then, the world will so accept the doctrines of
Satan that millions will march to their death in a futile attempt to make war against God. Millions have already died
for a false ideology. Millions more will die for the same insane reason.

What is this satanic ideology that will devastate the
lives of men? We find the answer in the first chapter of
Job, on the occasion where the sons of God stood before
the Lord.

> Now there was a day when the sons of God came to pre-
> sent themselves before the Lord, and Satan came also
> among them. And the Lord said unto Satan, Whence co-
> mest thou? Then Satan answered the Lord, and said,

From going to and fro in the earth, and from walking up and down in it. And the Lord said unto Satan, Hast thou considered my servant Job, that there is none like him in the earth, a perfect and an upright man, one that feareth God, and escheweth evil? Then Satan answered the Lord, and said, Doth Job fear God for nought? (Job 1:6-9)

"Does Job fear God for nothing?" states the devil's fourth doctrine. This satanic question implies the inner core of the infernal ideology that motivated the rebellion of Satan against God. Satan in effect is saying, "No one who is free to do otherwise will ever serve God except for what he gets out of it. Therefore, God is not worthy to rule the universe and is not intrinsically deserving of love and loyalty from anyone. Only mercenaries will do His bidding. Men will appear to serve God but only because of the temporal reward, not because He invites their loyalty."

Only mercenaries will serve Him! Here Satan delivers the most obscene insult possible before the throne of God. He attacks the very quality of the Godhead and implies that no person will do what is right just because it is right and godly but only because it is materially profitable. He asserts that only the temporal is significant; the divine and the eternal have no significance. God is not worthy to rule the universe, and He retains control only because He was there first! He, by accident of chronological priority, has the material resources to pay off unwilling and untrusting subjects. No one will serve God who is free to do otherwise.

We can learn a valuable lesson from this satanic statement, for from this question, we receive a clue as to the purpose for which man was created in the first place. When Lucifer declared himself against God, he set up a polarity of truth in the universe. He accused God of being unjust. God could, of course, have insisted on His justice. However, under His own rules, He must have a witness to that justice. The purpose, then, for the creation of man is to witness to the justice of God, to prove by his life and loyalty, that God is just and *intrinsically* worthy. We are here to prove that God is true. Satan revolted against this principle; therefore man was created. We were put into the devil's own territory to prove the most fundamental fact of the universe: God is true; God is just!

Who is this God whose truth and justice is being assaulted by this fourth satanic doctrine? This is the high and holy eternal being who is the ground of all other being. He is the One who is before all things and who has created all things by His eternal Son, the Lord Jesus Christ. He has revealed many characteristics about Himself in Holy Scripture, the sum of which gives us a truly awesome picture of this magnificent Father of all things who is our God. Let us notice some of the awesome statements of Scripture concerning the nature of our God. He is declared by the Word of God to be:

- Glorious (Exodus 15:11)
- Merciful (Exodus 34:6-7)
- Compassionate (2 Kings 13:23)
- Righteous (Ezra 9:15)
- Invisible (Job 23:8-9; Colossians 1:15)
- Upright (Psalm 25:8)
- Eternal (Psalm 90:2)
- Holy (Psalm 99:9)
- Immutable (Psalm 102:27)
- Gracious (Psalm 116:5)
- Good (Psalm 119:68)
- Omniscient (Psalm 139:1-6)
- Omnipresent (Psalm 139:7)
- Unsearchable (Psalm 145:3)
- Omnipotent (Jeremiah 32:17)
- Perfect (Matthew 5:48)
- Incorruptible (Romans 1:23)
- Wise (Romans 16:27)
- Faithful (1 Corinthians 10:13)

- Immortal (1 Timothy 1:17)
- Love (1 John 4:8, 16)

We are also told that He fills the heaven and earth (1 Kings 8:27; Jeremiah 23:24). This is therefore the God who should be worshiped with the total loyalty and allegiance of His creatures (John 4:24). God is just; God is good; He is the ultimate perfection of all things. When we realize these facts about God, we begin to sense how horrible and unspeakable was the assault against such a Person attempted by His prime minister, Satan. It seems unthinkable that a created being would attempt to insult the personality and integrity in so sublime a being. Satan, in his arrogance, has raised a question that reveals his fundamental ideology. The question, "Will a man serve God for nought?" is probably the most insulting question in all the history of the universe.

This satanic doctrine has important implications for us. The basic fact of the universe is that God is love and truth. Therefore, every person who does what is right—no matter what the consequence—commits the witness of his life in favor of God and against the devil. Every person who tells the truth despite the absence or impossibility of material reward is functioning as an individual made in the image of God.

Satan has asserted that God, in His essential being, is not worthy to be the absolutely prior Person in the universe. Satan espouses the false doctrine that ultimate truth and the final value of the universe is resident in some other place or person beside the Godhead. He suggests that God is able to create only an artificial magnetism or loyalty toward Himself because of His gifts and not because of the finality of His Person.

Ultimate truth, according to the devil, is not in God Himself. Because of this, he advances the argument that a person's final motivation will be within himself, not within the Person of his God. He advocates the notion that we will not commit ourselves to truth in the objective sense, but only to an alternate object which is our final truth, or profit. He suggests that the objective truth of God is a sham and that no person will in any way commit himself to it except for personal profit. Final truth, therefore, is not resident in God, but it is resident in personal advantage.

Once again, the proper conduct of our lives, if we are to live to the honor of our God, has to do with our relationship to this word *truth*. Our lives are godly or satanic, depending on whether we do or do not commit ourselves to the existence of an objective value outside of ourselves. When we deny the doctrine of objective value, we have denied the very ground of our being, and we must produce our personal destruction and finally the abolition of humanity. The question reduces itself to the final one, Is objective value in God or in ourselves? Will we commit ourselves to a truth that is outside of ourselves, even if that commitment produces personal disadvantage?

Our parents' expression "Tell the truth and shame the devil!" is not a superficial slogan but is rather the wisest possible advice that any of us can receive. Truth is the substance out of which the universe is made, and it really represents the essential nature of reality. Therefore, words like *truth, integrity, honor*, and *justice* are the most important words in any language. They must be embraced with the deepest commitment by any person who would shame the devil by refuting his doctrine.

Truth is so greatly emphasized in the Bible because it is so representative of God Himself. He is called "the true God" (2 Chronicles 15:3). He gives us "true laws" (Nehemiah 9:13). His Word is "true from the beginning" (Psalm 119:160). "A true witness delivereth souls" (Proverbs 14:25). Jesus Christ is the truth (John 14:6; Matthew 22:16). He is the "true Light" (John 1:9). He is the "true bread" (John 6:32). He is the "true vine" (John 15:1), and He is the only true way to the God of truth (1 John 5:20).

God solidly identifies Himself with truth. Therefore, he who is on the side of truth is on the side of God.

How shall we respond to this truth, which is the basis of the universe? We are told to "draw near with a true heart" (Hebrews 10:22) and to meditate on "whatsoever things are true" (Philippians 4:8). God "desires truth in the inward parts" (Psalm 51:6) and promises that truth will be our shield (Psalm 91:4). God says that His truth endures forever (Psalm 117:2) and advises us always to choose the way of truth (Psalm 119:30). We are to speak the truth, do the truth, live the truth, and be guided by the Spirit of truth (John 16:13). We are finally warned of the impossibility of succeeding in any other course of action. "We can do nothing against the truth, but for the truth" (2 Corinthians 13:8). Therefore, Scripture well advises, "Buy the truth, and sell it not" (Proverbs 23:23).

By contrast, we are reminded that Satan is a liar from the beginning, that there is no truth in him. Because he rejected the pillar and ground of truth, namely the Person of God Himself, Satan became a murderer and a deceiver, the embodiment of all that is untrue.

When Satan asserts that God is not worthy in Himself to rule the universe and therefore the standard of our lives must be the some other than God's truth, he is describing the tragic situation in our present world. How many millions live a lie; that is, they live for some reason other than loyalty to truth, to the Person of God Himself? Every person who lives primarily for material gain, pleasure, applause, even altruism, is committing himself to a principle that is essentially satanic.

Satan asserts that no one will serve God for Himself alone but only for a more immediate reward. He wants us to believe that ultimate reality lies not in the Person of God Himself but rather in one of the rewards that comes from Him. It follows therefore that those who serve God for merely human reward are doing the devil's work.

The life of every person is built on a first principle. If

that first principle is something other than the intrinsic worth of God Himself, that life is oriented in a satanic direction. Before the throne of God, Satan attacks this first principle and declares that no one will serve God for Who He is, only for what he can get out of it.

God will only be served by those who profit from it. How broadly is the satanic doctrine being practiced? It is frightening to contemplate the extent to which this devilish heresy has influenced the course of many.

We who live in this confused religious scene do well to be warned from the Word of God concerning the religious mercenaries, those who presumably serve God but are actually dedicated to material gain. In the name of God, some have separated trusting souls from their money, and in the process, promoted personal wealth through religious exploitation. Their clever promises and adroit manipulations have led distressed and needy souls to press money into their hands that should have gone to buy food for their families. These religious promoters promise blessing, healing, even prosperity, but not without a stated or strongly implied price. The ministry of some is well described by Paul in his warning to Timothy. He describes their message as "Perverse disputings of men of corrupt minds, and destitute of the truth, supposing that gain is godliness: from such withdraw thyself" (1 Timothy 6:5). I find it hard to believe that some religious promoters serve the same Jesus who said, "The foxes have holes, and the birds of the air have nests; but the Son of man hath not where to lay his head" (Matthew 8:20).

For them, it is almost as if the Bible did not say, "Lay not up for yourselves treasures upon earth, where moth and rust doth corrupt, and where thieves break through and steal: But lay up for yourselves treasures in heaven, where neither moth nor rust doth corrupt, and where thieves do not break through nor steal: for where your treasure is, there will your heart be also" (Matthew 6:19-21). Many today are hard put to remember, "The love of money is the root of all evil" (1 Timothy 6:10), and, "In the world ye shall have tribulation" (John 16:33), and, "Unto you it is given in the behalf of Christ, not only to believe on him, but also to suffer for his sake" (Philippians 1:29).

In opposition to this doctrine of Satan, let us remember the correct biblical view. Material things are to be used to the glory of God. Material things are morally neutral, but they take on spiritual significance when they are invested in the things that count for eternity. Happy is the person who exercises both the wisdom and the discipline to use material things for an eternal purpose rather than the satisfaction of his own indulgences. It takes a wise and disciplined man to lay up for himself treasures in heaven. Our hierarchy of values was well stated by our Lord Jesus Christ when He commanded us, "Seek ye first the kingdom of God, and his righteousness; and all these things shall be added unto you" (Matthew 6:33).

To take any other course puts us in spiritual danger. Material things can move up in our order of values so that they become, first, the object of our interest, then fascination, then love. It is at this point that we become materialists; beguiled away from our first devotion to God by the incursion of temporal things. At this point we violate the Scripture that admonishes us, "Love not the world, neither the things that are in the world. If any man love the world, the love of the Father is not in him" (1 John 2:15).

The church in the Western world should well heed the instances in Scripture where material things grew up to turn the people of God away from the purpose of God. This was the story in the history of the nation of Israel and was the reason for the recurring judgment from God upon this nation. The history of the church also brings us the tragic, recurring story of repeated spiritual treason by the religious establishment. Virtually every church or religious movement begins with dedicated people who give the total of their spiritual and material powers, even unto death, to advance the kingdom of Christ. Then the classic story unfolds. Dedication produces success, and success, prosperity. Prosperity then inevitably diminishes spiritual fervor, and the hand of the blessing of God is lifted from a once fruitful spiritual effort.

Is this not the precise story of the last of the seven churches of the Revelation?

> And unto the angel of the church of the Laodiceans write; These things saith the Amen, the faithful and true witness, the beginning of the creation of God; I know thy works, that thou art neither cold nor hot: I would thou wert cold or hot. So then because thou art lukewarm, and neither cold nor hot, I will spue thee out of my mouth. Because thou sayest, I am rich, and increased with goods, and have need of nothing; and knowest not that thou art wretched; and miserable, and poor, and blind, and naked: I counsel thee to buy of me gold tried in the fire, that thou mayest be rich; and white raiment, that thou mayest be clothed, and that the shame of thy nakedness do not appear; and anoint thine eyes with eyesalve, that thou mayest see. As many as I love, I rebuke and chasten: be zealous therefore, and repent. (Revelation 3:14-19)

It would be interesting to note the reception in our present churches to the words of the prophet Amos, were he to speak in our time as he spoke to the wealthy and lethargic of Israel before their destruction and captivity.

> Woe to them that are at ease in Zion. . . . That lie upon beds of ivory, and stretch themselves upon their couches, and eat the lambs out of the flock, and the calves out of the midst of the stall; that chant to the sound of the viol, and invent to themselves instruments of music, like David; that drink wine in bowls, and anoint themselves with the chief ointments: but they are not grieved for the affliction of Joseph. Therefore

now shall they go captive with the first that go captive, and the banquet of them that stretched themselves shall be removed. The Lord God hath sworn by himself, saith the Lord the God of hosts, I abhor the excellency of Jacob, and hate his palaces: therefore will I deliver up the city with all that is therein. (Amos 6:1, 4-8)

Satan has done a most notable work in the religious establishment of our world. He has often turned the eyes of the faithful from service to Jesus Christ because of Who Christ is. As an alternative, he has given us many related human reasons that have become the motives for which we live. This day of spiritual crisis may be an appropriate moment for a personal inventory as to what motivates us to serve Christ.

Satan still raises the most relevant question, "Doth Job fear God for nothing?" We can rejoice in the fact that the life of Job, that distinguished servant of God, became a sterling refutation of this satanic doctrine. Remembering this, we should pray that our lives may refute the devil's falsehoods as well. A good question to ask ourselves is, "What have I done today that makes my life a serious threat to Satan and his kingdom?"

6

"Adversity Must Produce Apostasy"

Satan's fifth doctrine is stated in the devil's continuing speech before God as he contemptuously discusses the situation of Job, that righteous servant of God. "Hast not thou made a hedge about him, and about his house, and about all that he hath on every side? thou hast blessed the work of his hands, and his substance is increased in the land. But put forth thine hand now, and touch all that he hath, and he will curse thee to thy face" (Job 1:10-11). In other words, no man will face human adversity without crumbling into bitterness and cursing his God.

What an insult to humanity!

Here, our enemy goes a step beyond his fourth doctrine, that no one will serve God except for human rewards. He is now insisting that no one will stay true to his presumed allegiance to a heavenly Father if he must face adverse and distressing circumstances as he lives his life. The absence of gain is one thing; real loss is quite another.

This implies that a man who is overtaken by intolerable reverses and divested of his human resources will forsake the Lord. He will blame God for his problems. The satanic assertion is that no one will believe in the goodness and love of God no matter what happens to him. God must always prove His love with sunshine and flowers. He must embody it in material substance for it to be real. He must never allow a person to suffer who serves Him, for suffering will produce infidelity.

The subtle suggestion is, therefore, that the love of God, His grace, and mercy are not real attributes of His being but are only God's patronizing activities. They are real only when visible and when producing pleasing and benign circumstances. There is no person, Satan insists, who will remain confident in the love of God because it is an intrinsic part of the nature of God. Rather, he will believe only when that love produces profitable things for him. The evil one insists that the evidence of the love of God is sight, not faith.

This satanic doctrine denies sound Christian doctrine. The basis of God's working with men in all ages is that "the just shall live by faith" (Romans 1:17). The Bible declares that faith is itself the substance of things hoped for; it is itself the evidence of things that we do not see (Hebrews 11:1). It follows that faith is not faith merely when it is confirmed by our cooperating circumstances. Indeed, the Scripture teaches that faith is faith only when it is operating in contrast to our circumstances. The moment that there is a change in our untoward circumstances and the results of faith become apparent, then faith is no longer operative. "For what a man seeth, why doth he yet hope for?" (Romans 8:24). Satan denies all this, suggesting that there is really no such thing as faith; confidence is built on sight alone. He does not merely redefine faith; he denies its very existence.

So important was it that this satanic doctrine be refuted that the Lord gave Satan every opportunity to oppress Job to the breaking point, if he could.

> And the Lord said unto Satan, Behold, all that he hath is in thy power; only upon himself put not forth thine hand. So Satan went forth from the presence of the Lord. And there was a day when his sons and his daughters were eating and drinking wine in their eldest broth-

er's house: and there came a messenger unto Job, and said, The oxen were plowing, and the asses feeding beside them: and the Sabeans fell upon them, and took them away; yea, they have slain the servants with the edge of the sword; and I only am escaped alone to tell thee. While he was yet speaking, there came also another, and said, The fire of God is fallen from heaven, and hath burned up the sheep, and the servants, and consumed them; and I only am escaped alone to tell thee. (Job 1:12-16)

These frightening reverses continue.

While he was yet speaking, there came also another, and said, The Chaldeans made out three bands, and fell upon the camels, and have carried them away, yea, and slain the servants with the edge of the sword; and I only am escaped alone to tell thee. While he was yet speaking, there came also another, and said, Thy sons and thy daughters were eating and drinking wine in their eldest brother's house: and, behold, there came a great wind from the wilderness, and smote the four corners of the house, and it fell upon the young men, and they are dead; and I only am escaped alone to tell thee. Then Job arose, and rent his mantle, and shaved his head, and fell down upon the ground, and worshipped. (Job 1:17-20)

Here is the story of a string of personal tragedies that fell upon the life of a servant of God, the equal of which will rarely befall any man. If ever there was a person who would be able to prove from the evidence of his external circumstances that he was the object of divine hatred, it was the patriarch Job. His world had fallen apart, and he had nothing left but a heap of ashes, a nagging wife, and three philosopher "friends" to complicate matters.

What was Job's response to all of this? Did he throw up his hands and deny the Lord? The answer is, of course, that he did not. Being absolutely sure of the love and the providence of God, he made another one of his great statements of faith, "Naked came I out of my mother's womb, and naked shall I return thither: the Lord gave, and the Lord hath taken away; blessed be the name of the Lord. In all this Job sinned not, nor charged God foolishly" (Job 1:21-22). It is beautiful to see the satanic theology that adversity must bring spiritual denial devastatingly repudiated in the life and testimony of Job. Job became the classic illustration of the truth that alone can help the individual to say in the midst of changing times, "The just shall live by faith."

Few of us will be able to resist the temptation to believe Satan's non-faith theology unless we understand the real nature of faith in a Christian sense. The faith of the Christian, his belief in the existence and goodness of God, is not a temporary attitude that he musters from time to time in this life. One's view is childish if he believes that faith is something that he exercises all weekend, knowing he will see the glad fulfillment of his faith on Monday morning. Our faith is not like that. Faith, to the Christian, is a much higher thing, far above the level of ordinary human understanding.

It is higher because it believes totally in the existence and goodness of God who is above and beyond nature and therefore "by the very nature of things," must not reveal Himself in nature any more than He does. To manifest Himself through nature more, God would have to destroy it. So long, then, as we are in a natural world, it is not possible for us to prove empirically that our faith is true. Only beyond this life, when we step from nature into supernature, will we move beyond the need for faith. Until then, faith must be the basis for our very life. In saying, "The just shall live by faith," God means faith will be the very basis of our existence and that will be the case for all of our natural lives. Again, we must insist that this is how things are in the natural realm. For God to prove Himself to be as big and as powerful as our faith tells us He is, He would have to destroy the universe.

Within the order of creation, there are no eyes that can truly behold God's face; there is no heart that can truly appreciate God's love; there is no mind that can comprehend the breadth of God's wisdom. "As the heavens are higher than the earth, so are my ways higher than your ways, and my thoughts than your thoughts" (Isaiah 55:9). Paul declares, "Who hath known the mind of the Lord? or who hath been his counsellor?" (Romans 11:34). Not while we are in this life will we move beyond the necessity of living by faith. Therefore, so long as we live, we will be vulnerable to the satanic argument that our only course is to despair, that faith in an unseen God is foolish. There is no way that it can ever be different, for there is no way that the supernatural can fully reveal itself within the natural. God has so constituted nature that it is almost impossible to see the supernatural in it at all, except through the eyes of faith.

Almost, but not quite. The "not quite" is what Christianity is all about. The fact is that God in His wisdom did find a way to reveal a measure of the glory of His Person within the natural world. He did find a way to bring before the eyes of faith some factual evidence of His existence and His love.

How do we know that God loves us? Is it because of health and strength and wealth and plentiful supply? What is the real evidence of the love of God? On what basis can we still believe in the love of our heavenly Father when we live in the midst of war, poverty, privation, and a multitude of human reverses? What minister of the gospel has not been asked the question, "If God is love, why is there so much suffering in the world?"

Really now, how do we know that God loves us? The answer is that He reached into nature and made Himself and His love an observable thing in the lives of men. We know that God loves us because Christ came into the world. He lived and died on the cross to save us from our sins. "Herein is love, not that we loved God, but that He loved us, and sent His Son to be the propitiation for our sins" (1 John 4:10). Again, "God commendeth His love toward us, in that, while we were yet sinners, Christ died for us" (Romans 5:8). So it is that the Christian, having accepted the love of God in Jesus Christ as being the final evidence of the tender care of our heavenly Father, is refuting this doctrine of the devil.

The proof of the love of God in our lives is not sunshine and flowers. It is the historical fact of the death of Jesus Christ and the present indwelling of His Spirit in our lives. The reality of Jesus Christ is what makes it possible to trust God when we are facing the storms of life. Circumstances, to the Christian, having nothing to do with the question of the reality of the love of God. Prosperity, of itself, does not prove that God is for us, and adversity is no final indication that God has forsaken us.

The testimony of Job should forever settle the fact that our physical happenings are not of themselves spiritually significant. He "sendeth rain on the just and on the unjust" (Matthew 5:45).

"Don't doubt in the darkness what God has told you in the light" is good advice indeed! The events of our lives certainly will not always cooperate for our pleasure. There must inevitably be times when we pass through darkness in which there seems to be no light whatsoever. Prayers are not always answered in the precise shape of our expectations. Needs are not always supplied with the specifications that we demand of God. Things do not always work together for good in an empirically provable sense. An old Arab proverb says, "God writes straight with crooked lines." One of the most obvious facts of life is that God does not run His rivers like arrows down to the sea. The evidence of the love and tender care of our heavenly Father cannot be based upon our cooperating and rewarding environment.

A moment's reflection, however, will quickly remind us that only a fool would believe the satanic doctrine that momentary events prove faith foolish. We all know that too much sunshine will create a desert. Rain is also needed to cool the earth, irrigate the fields, and even to furnish a bit of rewarding variation from the sameness of eternal sunshine. We also know that many times, a ship has traveled faster through the storm than it had through the calm seas.

Therefore, most people would do well to change their attitudes about this whole question of adversity and problems, lest they become very weak-minded in their whole outlook on life. Many of us are too soon discouraged, too easily crushed. We burst into tears when faced with the slightest difficulties. Our weak "sunshine faith" is much too readily demolished. We need to heed again the stern admonition of Scripture:

> For consider him that endured such contradiction of sinners against himself, lest ye be wearied and faint in your minds. Ye have not yet resisted unto blood, striving against sin. And ye have forgotten the exhortation which speaketh unto you as unto children. My son, despise not thou the chastening of the Lord, nor faint when thou art rebuked of him: For whom the Lord loveth he chasteneth, and scourgeth every son whom he receiveth. If ye endure chastening, God dealeth with you as with sons; for what son is he whom the father chasteneth not? But if ye be without chastisement, whereof all are partakers, then are ye bastards, and not sons. (Hebrews 12:3-8)

If we would take a moment for reflection and firm up our attitudes, we may move to a whole new and exciting level of life. Indeed, a man is a fool if when in trouble, he neglects to stop, think, and remind himself that problems are themselves the price of progress. We must remember that the word *problem* is simply a description of our reaction to an event; it is not a denotation of the event itself. A wrinkled fender may be a "problem" to the person who is driving the automobile, but for the person who operates the body shop, it is an opportunity. Many of our words are really descriptions of our own personal attitudes, rather than objective definitions of our environment.

What may be a storm to one person is simply a refreshing rain to another. It therefore follows that a hateful and bitter reaction to one's circumstances is quite stupid. A second, considered, analytical look at a pile of rubble may suggest many golden possibilities to the creative mind, if that mind will take a moment for reflection rather than reacting in despair.

Contemplation or reaction, what a difference there is between the two! Indeed, one may be divine and the other satanic. Satan, in his fifth doctrine, implies that man, as a mere human animal, will only react to his circumstances. He suggests that man's response to difficulty will be instantaneous and negative rather than rational, considerate, and reflective. Satan hopes that all of us will live our lives on the basis of action and reaction rather than reflective thinking. Hoping for an emotional response, he will constantly push us to panic rather than allow us to take a moment for reflection. Satan would have us believe that we react rather than think, attributing to man a violent, animalistic stupidity in saying, "Touch all that he hath, and he will curse thee to thy face."

Who of us has not seen this satanic drive work in our lives? What man has not, in the heat of anger, fear, or disappointment, been tempted to say or do something for which he was soon sorry? Most of the sins of our lives would have been avoided with just a moment's reflection. Has not the experience of life taught us that our instant reaction to our circumstances has almost always been wrong? I am not speaking, of course, about leaping away from a speeding automobile or reflexively avoiding a collision when driving. Rather, I am suggesting that it is almost impossible to *analyze* instantly a complex set of circumstances and to make the correct moral decision in a flash.

Job himself is an illustration of this. He did not react to the loss of his wealth by cursing God. He took time to think, to consider, and even to discuss at length all of these things with his philosopher friends. Even though their advice was not the most encouraging, nevertheless, the fact of the discussion surely helped Job to spread his emotions over a longer period of days. He did not curse God to His face, as Satan said he would. He was saved from this by taking time to think about it.

A moment's reflection may also change our view of our circumstances. Who has not discovered that, when carefully analyzed, practically any problem is not really so disastrous as it appeared to be at first?

With this in mind, I spoke recently to a friend of mine and asked, "Have the problems of life that you have faced through the years usually turned out to be greater or less than what you originally expected them to be?" He answered, smiling in knowing fashion, as if appreciating the relevance of the question, "Practically without exception, my problems have been less of a difficulty than initially I expected them to be."

For many of us, a moment's contemplation on the love of God plus an extra moment to think through our circumstances would prevent us from falling into an agreement with Satan that personal loss is grounds to curse the Lord.

To help develop the right attitude, let sink deeply into your firmest convictions the beautiful definition of God found in Scripture, "God is love" (1 John 4:8). How reassuring it is to the soul to remember that "I have loved thee with an everlasting love" (Jeremiah 31:3); "his banner over me was love" (Song of Solomon 2:4); "greater love hath no man than this, that a man lay down his life for his friends" (John 15:13); and "to know the love of Christ, which passeth knowledge" (Ephesians 3:19). We need to be moved again by the blessed recollection that Jesus Christ, "having loved his own . . . he loved them unto the end" (John 13:1). On the basis of this marvelous data, we are confident that the promise of God is true, that since God be for us, who can be against us? (Romans 8:31).

A proper understanding of the love of God will assure us that He is for us no matter what may be our momentary circumstances. Our faith that God is for us is based on a proper estimate of His goodness and the consequent confidence that His promises do not fail. Out with circumstances; up with Scripture!

The devil would bend all of his powers to destroy this faith. He knows that every person who loves God no matter what is confirming the basic fact of the universe, namely, that God is just and He is also love. It is utterly important that we remain true to the Lord despite any degree of pain and problems that we may face. Life will, for most of us, be characterized by temporary periods of prosperity and adversity. In good times, we probably can impress an onlooking world with our prosperity as being an evidence of the blessing of God. But our faith will impress people even more if we are strong in the Lord when we are passing through a time of want or even the valley of the shadow of death.

The person who, because of the temporary dislocation of his affairs, denies that a gracious God is working on his behalf, is committing himself to the satanic doctrine of a loveless, unjust God. The Christian whose circumstances produce the cry that "God has forsaken me" has slipped into dangerous, sub-Christian thinking. About the early heroes of the faith, the hymn writer said,

> They climbed the steep ascent of heaven,
> Through peril, toil and pain;
> Oh, God to us let grace be given
> To follow in their train.

God is just. God is love. Job never doubted it. Satanic subversion is constantly at work to deny individuals the glorious freedom that comes from faith in these blessed certainties.

7

"This Life Is Everything"

What is life all about? One of the most elaborate discussions in all of literature centered around this most relevant question is found in the book of Job. Like each of us today, Job, his wife, and their philosopher friends were people looking for answers.

Job had participated in all the joys and sorrows that can come to an individual through human experience. He knew about family life, personal riches, fulfillment, and all that the world could offer. Personal tragedy and the loss of all things followed those green years, precipitating the discussion that we find in this most exciting book of the Old Testament. The book of Job is the great treatise in the Bible that seeks for meaning in human experience. The discussion in the book of Job was caused by the heavenly scene where Satan pressed his sixth doctrine before the throne of God. Satan's sixth doctrine is the pernicious suggestion that *this life is everything*.

The biblical account as to how all of this took place is frightening as well as thrilling.

> Again there was a day when the sons of God came to present themselves before the Lord, and Satan came also among them to present himself before the Lord.

And the Lord said unto Satan, From whence comest thou? And Satan answered the Lord, and said, From going to and fro in the earth, and from walking up and down in it. And the Lord said unto Satan, Hast thou considered my servant Job, that there is none like him in the earth, a perfect and an upright man, one that feareth God, and escheweth evil? and still he holdest fast his integrity, although thou movedst me against him, to destroy him without cause. And Satan answered the Lord, and said, Skin for skin, yea, all that a man hath will he give for his life. But put forth thine hand now, and touch his bone and his flesh, and he will curse thee to thy face. And the Lord said unto Satan, Behold, he is in thine hand; but save his life. So went Satan forth from the presence of the Lord, and smote Job with sore boils from the sole of his foot unto his crown. And he took him a potsherd to scrape himself withal; and he sat down among the ashes. (Job 2:1-8)

Job's friends, when they heard of the great evil that had come upon Job, gathered to try to find a reason, an interpretation of the events of his life.

One of the primary messages of this Old Testament masterpiece is the lesson that experiences by themselves teach us nothing. We can never be sure, merely from the knowledge that comes to us by experience, that at any given moment we are being blessed or cursed of God. There is no event in our lives and no related joy or sorrow that can tell us by itself whether there is any meaning to life or any reason for the concerns of this moment. Knowing this, Job and his friends talk together about that most important question. What is the meaning of life? Life is something deeper than experiences themselves. The physical event can only be understood when the spiritual event related to it becomes apparent.

This fact of life often escapes us. Too many people point to physical events in their lives and the experiences that they produce as proving something about God and spiritual reality. This is most dangerous thinking. All physical events, all emotions, all experiences are strictly limited to the human level. None of these events have meaning in themselves. They can become meaningful to us only if we have some kind of insight from God. They can be understood only when we are able to view the heavenly scene.

We could not have understood the reason for the experience of Job, were we not given the opportunity of looking into heaven and viewing the scene before the throne of his Father. We probably would have agreed that surely God had forsaken Job. Even the conversations of the book of Job itself answer few of the questions that are posted in this philosophic discussion. Most of these questions go unanswered in the Old Testament. They are only answered by Christ in the New Testament when He brought life and immortality to light through the gospel. The reasonings of the philosophers do not answer the problems of men. The Word of God gives us the only possible solution to questions posed as to the meaning of life.

The primary question in the book of Job really centers on the basic concern of all philosophy, namely, Do the events of life have a meaning that is larger than life itself? Is there something more basic than what seems apparent and understandable to our finite minds? Does reality have a deeper nature than what we can see with our eyes? Is there a *life* that is more important than this physical existence? Does an understanding of that life explain and unravel the problems of this one? Satan would have us believe that the answer is no! According to his doctrine this life is everything.

The true answer is just the opposite. It is, yes, a thousand times, yes! In denying the existence of a life more primary and more important than this, Satan reveals his sixth doctrine, "This life is everything." This satanic subversion is summed up in his words, "Skin for skin, yea, all that a man hath will he give for his life. But put forth thine hand now, and touch his bone and his flesh, and he will curse thee to thy face" (Job 2:4-5).

What a statement! Here Satan is delivering his lowest, most demeaning insult to humanity, which was made in the image of God. He says that man has no divine likeness and insists that he will esteem his physical life as the treasure most worth preserving. He suggests that man will give up his money, betray his friends, sell his soul, and throw away his integrity if, in the process, he can preserve his life. *Integrity* is an important word. Job's wife understood some of the issues in speaking with him, saying, "Dost thou still retain thine integrity? Curse God, and die" (Job 2:9).

Let us consider this satanic doctrine that physical life is the highest good and that every moral and spiritual value is to be sacrificed for the preservation of human, animal existence. A moment's reflection will remind us of how much of our modern world is built on the satanic assumption of the all-importance of physical life and the things pertaining to it. Life must be preserved, indulged, made comfortable, exalted, and even worshiped! This is the basic proposition that prevails as the undergirding of modern thought and action. Here is materialism at its fullest flower. Man is merely atoms and molecules; he has no continuing existence. The preservation of this life, therefore, even though it demands the sacrifice of all other values, is the only wise course for the individual to follow.

Is this philosophy practiced in our day? Indeed it is. Many seemingly sincere people announce the first principle of their thinking that life must be preserved at all costs. By this, they mean that physical existence is all there is and therefore obviously the thing most worth saving. They become ecologists, politicians, demonstrators, naturalists, yogas, gurus, or simply preoccupied with this life as if there were no other. They lend their time and talent to this world's legitimate and illegitimate professions. Together, they have built this vast edifice called society, a

remarkable organism that is beautiful to behold, external-
ly attractive but internally corrupt. Its corruption is implicit in its basic assumption, namely that final value is
found in this human existence. Almost all magazines,
books, professions, institutions, and activities are dedicated to the principle that this life is the only life we know or
can know. *Materialism* is the name for all of this, and materialism is the religion of this world. Another of its names
is *humanism*. Satan is the founder of that faith.

Make no mistake about it. Materialism is not just another possible point of view, but a most deadly philosophy
that can issue in murderous activity. When one is a materialist and interprets every value according to the con-
stricted logic of this human life, he can say with the
Communists that man is merely a human animal; he is atoms in motion. He has no value except in terms of his relationship with society, and all truth, all purpose, is
measured as practical or impractical in terms of its value
to society. Millions have been murdered in the name of
this philosophy, and millions more will be swept from the
face of the earth by this religion called materialism. While
professing interest in man, materialism is really willing to
destroy man in order to "save mankind."

It is somewhat surprising that in the face of this philosophy, we have so many activities, which seem damaging
to this life, which we hold to be of such value. The rising
practice and acceptance of abortion is a good illustration
of one of the twisted values of humanism. In the last ten
years, 20 percent of America's innocent unborn died at
the hand of the abortionist. Statistics report 40 million an-
nual abortions worldwide.

Why did those children die? They died because of
this generation's godless ideology—humanism. When the
humanist says this life is everything, he means this moment, this hour of life. He does not consider the perpetua-
tion of life into future generations. When an issue
becomes unpleasant or inconvenient, it is made to disap-

pear, whatever the cost in the future.

Another interesting corollary to total materialism in our world is the rise of suicide. If this life is the final and highest good, then when it becomes finally intolerable, it is perfectly logical (from one point of view) to end it. Such was the reasoning of the sixty-five-year-old former movie star who took his own life, saying, "I am totally bored with everything about life, and there is nothing left for me to live for."

Job's wife, being a materialist, gave him the exactly this advice. She said, "Curse God, and die" (Job 2:9). How wonderful that we have the perceptive answer of that faithful man of God. "But he said unto her, Thou speakest as one of the foolish women speaketh. What? Shall we receive good at the hand of God, and shall we not receive evil? In all this did not Job sin with his lips" (Job 2:10). Here is one of the great statements in all of the Bible. "Shall we receive good at the hand of God, and shall we not receive evil?" With these words, Job is expressing his profound faith in the goodness of God, which faith is largely not told even by the religious movements of our generation.

Millions of untutored followers of Jesus Christ have come to believe the philosophy, rejected by Job and all of his faithful heirs, that blessing always takes the form of good and pleasurable things and never things that are inconvenient or painful. Surely Job would have been sickened at the emphasis of some today who would have us believe that only good things happen to us because we are followers of God. The religion that preaches that physical and material benefits are always the result of faith may be fascinating to the naive, but it is not the religion of the Bible. This argument usually comes from the fantasies of those who have deceived themselves and who would in turn deceive us.

The reason, of course, for the success of such deceivers is the fact that this satanic suggestion that this life is everything is believed by many. Almost everyone, as Satan suggested, will give all that he has for his life. The average individual can be counted upon to sacrifice treasure and even integrity for the promise of additional, comfortable years in this physical life. The almost truth of this doctrine of the devil is the promotional base that has made possible the cynical extraction of millions of dollars in exchange for false hope from many of the naive.

We may expect that this activity will increase. Since we have moved from the age of faith and the age of reason into the age of sight, we can expect that there will now break upon us the age of fantasy. When we begin believing in the final truth of that which we can see with our eyes, we are preparing ourselves for the deceivers who are planning to enrich themselves by exploiting us. Since we have redefined faith as now meaning "that state of mind that always produces good things," we have laid ourselves open to the exploits of the religious magicians and charlatans.

How tragic this tempting satanic doctrine has been for faithful people who have lived reliable, spiritual lives through most of their time in this world. They have enjoyed the blessing of God in sickness and in health; through prosperity and adversity, they have been faithful to the teaching of Scripture and the leadership of the Holy Spirit. Alas, then comes the final test. They are informed that they have an incurable disease for which no human remedy is known. A subtle new thought is introduced into their minds. They tell themselves, *Maybe it is just possible that the local or international miracle-worker can indeed produce a miracle and give me additional years of life.* This thought produces hope, and hope surges into fantasy, and, but for the sobering presence of the Holy Spirit, they chase off to a gathering in pursuit of the nonsense that physical life is eternally preservable. Through anxiety, desperation, and increasing impoverishment, they are cleverly led to expect a miracle. They become living illustrations of the almost truth of the devil's doctrine that everything that a person possesses he will give for his life.

Scriptural knowledge and good sense are cast aside, and the fool that lurks within us takes over. There is no verse in the Bible that, properly understood, guarantees a formula for certain healing or a predictable miracle. Not until Jesus Christ comes again will the bondage of corruption be lifted from suffering humanity. In the meantime, the wise Christian will learn to rest in the Lord and to trust that there is a scene in heaven that perfectly explains his present adversity. Weak faith looks for a miracle. Settled and biblical faith rests in the Lord, affirming, "Though he slay me, yet will I trust in him." It is settled faith that retains its integrity.

Must we go along with the satanic doctrine that "all a man hath will he give for his life?" The answer is no! Have there not been people who have been faithful unto death and who have never allowed their extreme physical circumstances to cause them to foolishly deny the faith that has supported them through life? Happily, the answer is yes. Saints down through history have proved by their faithfulness unto death that Satan is a liar. They have not given in to cynicism and despair in what they assumed to be the final pressures of this life. The father of all of these is Job. As an affirmation of his faith, he gives us one of the most marvelous statements of faith found in the Bible. It is Job's earnest affirmation of his utter confidence in the character of God. The pinnacle of all statements of confidence in God are the words of Job, "Though he slay me, yet will I trust in him."

Job understands faith in its correct sense. To him, faith is that confidence in the wisdom, justice, and love of God that is not to be forsaken, even in the most adverse circumstances. Job was confident that the plan of God was constantly working on his behalf, even though he himself would not be delivered from what appeared to be personal tragedy or physical death. His sense of the providence of God correctly concluded that the cooperating events of life or the absence of such events proved nothing as to the love and justice of God. Job must have sensed that there was a heavenly scene that could explain earthly events, and he knew that he would one day step into that heavenly scene. Faith sees the things that are invisible and is not so foolish as to demand that they become immediately visible. Faith is confident in heaven to come, and to faith, it is eternal life that makes this life explainable.

Implicit within this sixth satanic doctrine is the dismaying suggestion that there is no eternal life. Satan can greatly enhance the attractiveness of his doctrine that this life is everything, if he can lead us to believe that death is the end of existence and there is no possibility of a happy eternity with our heavenly Father. He has surely been devilishly active in putting the emphasis of modern philosophy—and even religious thought—upon this present world, to the point that millions doubt the reality of eternity. Our age has, as a result, become so worldly minded that any discussion of a life beyond this is considered quite ridiculous. "When you're dead, you're dead" is the philosophy of modern man. He refuses to discuss any alternate view, holding that there is no certainty about eternity.

Man therefore continues his desperate struggle to produce a utopia in this world, believing that his future on earth is the only future that there is. The materialists would have us believe that it is possible to create a perfect world. They refuse to remember that such plans have always failed. They also neglect to remind us that, even if a utopia were possible, we must still die and lose it all.

The preaching of this message and its related doctrines is one of Satan's clever activities. If we believe that this life is everything and that there is no eternity, we find ourselves in a trap. Experience teaches us that we lose this life, and if false doctrine also teaches us that there is no eternity, we must, if we are rational, be pressed to the point of despair. Despair is a great sin, and in producing it, Satan will have triumphed in our lives.

Is this life really everything? Is there real life beyond? Philosophy cannot answer these questions. No philosopher has ever given so much as one paragraph that answers the question, "If a man die, shall he live again?" The answers to the questions of eternity are only available to us from the Bible.

From those sacred pages, we see that eternity is so real and this life so transient that the Scripture says to the Christian, "If in this life only we have hope in Christ, we are of all men most miserable" (1 Corinthians 15:19). In the same passage, Paul declares that there is eternal life because Christ is risen from the dead and promises us that if we believe in Him, we shall rise from the dead as well. He promises a wonderful transformation on that occasion, declaring that the life to come will be infinitely better than the life that we know in this world.

> Behold, I shew you a mystery; we shall not all sleep, but we shall all be changed, in a moment, in the twinkling of an eye, at the last trump: for the trumpet shall sound, and the dead shall be raised incorruptible, and we shall be changed. For this corruptible must put on incorruption, and this mortal must put on immortality. So when this corruptible shall have put on incorruption, and this mortal shall have put on immortality, then shall be brought to pass the saying that is written, Death is swallowed up in victory. O death, where is thy sting? O grave, where is thy victory? The sting of death is sin; and the strength of sin is the law. But thanks be to God, which giveth us the victory through our Lord Jesus Christ. (1 Corinthians 15:51-57)

In many other places, the Bible gloriously affirms that there is life beyond this. In fact, the resurrection and the life hereafter become one of the grand themes of the Word of God. Jesus said, "Because I live, ye shall live also" (John 14:19). Paul talks about leaving this life, saying that he has "a desire to depart, and to be with Christ" (Philippians 1:23). He also says, "Our conversation is in heaven; from whence also we look for the Saviour, the Lord Jesus Christ" (Philippians 3:20). Again and again, the New Testament affirms the life beyond this. Finally, the Revelation states in a hundred ways the fact and the details of the heaven that awaits us when we believe Jesus Christ.

When we forget the sound doctrine of the certainty of heaven, we tend more quickly to make ourselves vulnerable to the satanic heresy that there is no eternal life. We therefore see the wisdom of Paul's admonition to "set your affection on things above, not on things on the earth" (Colossians 3:2). Satan has the greater difficulty subverting the Christian who has his eyes fixed upon his eternal destiny.

The church will be better able to survive the assault of satanic doctrine when it remembers that its ultimate destiny is in the reality of heaven. The question asked by Job's wife is relevant to the church and individual Christians today: "Dost thou still retain thine integrity?" Have we sold out in any degree to the doctrine of the devil? Has the object of our affection moved from eternity to time, from things that are spiritual to things that are material? Integrity is an important thing, and doctrinal integrity is the most important of all. Scripture teaches that integrity is worth more than life. Integrity, truth, and the righteousness of God are the very substance of the universe. Satanic theology insists that this point of view is foolish, but satanic theology will end in the same lake of fire that has long been prepared for the devil and his angels.

Has satanic doctrine infected the church in our day? Every fact and every proposition that is not true, even though it be believed in the most holy circles, is another ounce of leverage Satan can use against us. Satan's greatest work is not in demon possession or witchcraft. It is the introduction of false doctrine into the thinking of Christians, as a result of which they are rendered spiritually impotent.

The church of Christ is impotent to the precise degree that it has allowed the subversive doctrines of Satan rather than the truth of God to be the rule for its faith or practice. Satan's deadliest work is the production of false doctrine. The doctrine that Satan pushes that is perhaps the most false and nearly the most deadly is the idea that this human life is worth the sacrifice of all else.

Many things in the world are worth dying for: truth, integrity, and sound doctrine. When we no longer believe this, then the remainder of what we do believe is not worth believing.

8

"God Should
Work Miracles
on Demand"

One of the interesting developments on the current religious scene is the surge of interest in visible phenomena.
As people become increasingly disillusioned with the age
of materialism, they may well be approaching the attitude
of mind that Gideon had when, in a time of Israel's spiritual poverty, he remonstrated with God, "Oh, my Lord, if
the Lord be with us, why then is all this befallen us? And
where be all his miracles which our fathers told us of, saying, Did not the Lord bring us up from Egypt? But now the
Lord hath forsaken us, and delivered us into the hands of
the Midianites" (Judges 6:13).

"Where are all His miracles?" people who think of
themselves as the people of God often ask in a time of spiritual privation. In response to this sense of spiritual need,
there are increasing numbers of religious leaders and increasing masses of religious followers who claim that the
age of miracles has broken upon us in a new way. The
word *miracle* has reentered our vocabulary and has become an object of intense interest.

We sing songs about miracles, and many Christians
claim to have seen God work in miraculous ways. But, in
addition to this, we have miracle magazines, miracle
handkerchiefs, miracle publishing houses, miracle val-

leys, miracle messages, miracle meetings, and many who claim openly or by implication to have the gift of working one or another kind of miracles. This involvement has long been the case with the religious lunatic fringe, but extensive and loose talk about miracles has now entered into legitimate Christian circles.

This is therefore an appropriate time to note the seventh doctrine of the devil, namely, that God is a magician, working miracles on demand. We note this satanic doctrine from the account of Christ's temptation in the gospel of Matthew.

> Then was Jesus led up of the spirit into the wilderness to be tempted of the devil. And when he had fasted forty days and forty nights, he was afterward an hungered. And when the tempter came to him, he said, If thou be the Son of God, command that these stones be made bread. But he answered and said, It is written, Man shall not live by bread alone, but by every word that proceedeth out of the mouth of God. (Matthew 4:1-4)

In this passage, we have more than a dialogue between two individuals: this is the account of a stupendous moral contest, an encounter between good and evil, in which the destiny of the world was at stake. Here, Satan openly presents himself before Christ and presses his first temptation to the Savior, at what he presumes is Christ's greatest temporary vulnerability: physical hunger. For the past forty days, the Lord had eaten nothing, and food was not available. Knowing this, the wily adversary moves in with his first moral attack against Christ. He says, in effect, "If You are the Son of God, You have no problem with this matter of physical hunger. Be a magician; command that these stones be made bread." This suggests the satanic doctrine that working a miracle on demand is valid for the solution of personal problems and the satisfaction of physical needs. This implies that God is a magician, that a miracle is a capricious event, its purpose being temporary human satisfaction.

Christ's response to this satanic assertion is most instructive. "Man shall not live by bread alone, but by every word that proceedeth out of the mouth of God." He means that the physical or natural event is of itself without significance. The true significance of any phenomenon can only be understood by "every word that proceedeth out of the mouth of God." Reality, then, is not finally made out of atoms and molecules—out of bread alone. Reality is the Word of God; His Word is ultimate truth. Events, more miraculous ones, are not of themselves significant; significance lies in a knowledge and understanding of divine truth.

The many claims to mysterious, supernatural workings that are current today make imperative a re-examination of the marvel of the miraculous. The time has come to ask basic questions about miracles that are answered from the one reliable source of data, the Bible. After the experiences have been reported, the testimonies given, the songs sung, and the wheelchairs parked, we do well to look into the Word of God to discover what this current supernaturalistic talk is all about.

First of all, let us consider the word that is the center of the discussion, *miracle*. What is a miracle? *A miracle is a supernatural phenomenon in the experience of men, presumably occurring in contradiction to the laws of nature.*

By this definition, it is obvious that not everything that happens and not even everything that is unusual is a miracle. A real miracle must be something more than mere coincidence, an occurrence quite distinct from what we would expect of nature. Many wonderful events may take place in our lives, and we may call these answers to prayer and workings of God. We cannot, however, on this account, call them miracles. We need to be careful about using language in this regard.

This, of course, poses the second question: What is the proof of a miracle? We are warned in Scripture to "prove all things; hold fast that which is good" (1 Thessalonians 5:21). For want of proof, many naive and impressionable believers have been exploited by clever manipulators. Somehow, the idea that every claim of the unusual that comes to us with religious overtones must be believed, has entered into Christian thinking. Nothing could be further from the truth. The Bible warns us in many ways that the world will see false teachers (2 Peter 2:1) and is worked upon by liars, deceivers, and blasphemers, who, as we approach the end of the age, will grow worse and worse (2 Timothy 3:13). In the light of the mounting delusions of our present age (2 Thessalonians 2:11), we must take time to prove all things (1 Thessalonians 5:21).

We are enabled to do this if we will follow the rules of Scripture. Many passages in the Bible explain in detail the nature of proof. The first principle is that no one person's witness or testimony to an event is of itself proof at all. The law says, "One witness shall not rise up against a man for any iniquity, or for any sin, in any sin that he sinneth: at the mouth of two witnesses, or at the mouth of three witnesses, shall the matter be established" (Deuteronomy 19:15). The same principle of two or three witnesses is repeated in other places in the Old Testament (Numbers 35:30; Deuteronomy 17:6).

This rule for the verifying of unusual events was reestablished by Christ, saying, "That in the mouth of two or three witnesses every word may be established" (Matthew 18:16).

How, then, do we prove the truth of any event? Any occurrence or claim, event or accusation, must be established in the mouth of two, and better three, reliable witnesses. We must reemphasize the truthful aspect of it, for the Bible warns of the presence and danger of false witnesses.

With this in mind, we may ask a third question, What

is the purpose of a miracle? Obviously, the purpose of a miracle is not simply to do something interesting, nor merely to produce a result, such as healing, in the life of a person. It would be cruel for Christ to work a miracle for the sole object of producing healing in one and let others go without receiving this miracle. Happily, Scripture gives the purpose of the miracles of Christ.

The main purpose of Christ's miracles was to bear witness to the truth of revelation. Speaking of the great salvation that we have in the Lord Jesus, Scripture says, "Which at the first began to be spoken by the Lord, and was confirmed unto us by them that heard him; God also bearing them witnesses, both with signs and wonders, and with divers miracles, and gifts of the Holy Ghost, according to his own will?" (Hebrews 2:3-4). Clearly then, the purpose of miracles was to "bear them witness." God worked an unusual phenomenon in order to demonstrate to those present that Jesus Christ was the Son of God and that the word of the apostles was from God. The miracles were on-the-spot proof to the validity of a divine or divinely ordained speaker, either the Lord Jesus or the apostles.

If the purpose of a miracle is to bear witness to the truth of revelation, then obviously miracles are of little value when reported third or fourth hand, for soon they are spoken by individuals who cannot establish their credibility according to the law of evidence that we have stated. The verbal revelation of God, however, can be passed on from mind to mind and heart to heart. Truth bears its own credentials to the honest mind, especially when we remember that its early credentials were the miraculous power of God. The working of a miracle can be of great value to those who actually see it. The testimony of a miracle, passed on to others without the confirmation of eyewitnesses, loses that value. It is easy for the story to become confused, exaggerated, and easier yet for the listener to desire a similar miracle rather than to accept the truth of Scripture certified by the original miracle.

How unfortunate it is that so many reports are being published today of miracles from obscure corners of the world. Even if these remarkable events were true, it is unwise for them to be reported through books and pamphlets across the Christian world, because we cannot possibly prove their truth. There is no way you or I could assemble two or three competent witnesses to the miraculous occurrence. I must remember, therefore, that I am not required to believe these accounts; in fact, I am virtually required not to believe them. In that it is impossible for me to fulfill the admonition of Scripture to "prove all things," I must be careful not to let my mind be influenced by these phenomenalistic accounts of events that are contrary to nature.

Beside that, even if these events were true, they do not fulfill the purpose of miracles. The purpose of miracles in the New Testament was to be a witness, a certification by God, of the revelation of His Word. The revelation of the Word of God is now complete in the pages of Holy Scripture, and we are forbidden to add to or take away from the written, canonical revelation. The scriptural function of miracles has ceased, in that the written Word of God has already been certified with signs, wonders, miracles, and gifts of the Holy Spirit.

The publishing of these phenomenalistic accounts is not only pointless, it is also dangerous, because the naive reader has a tendency to ask, "If God is doing these things in other places, why don't I see such miraculous events?" This person understandably tends to make a universal doctrine out of what may be a specific and unrepeated working of God in a given place. The Word, therefore, that we are to spread across the world is not the unsupportable verbal accounts of "miraculous events" but the scriptural account of the great event that produced the gospel. This event, of course, is the death, burial, and resurrection of Christ.

Because of the many warnings in Scripture, we obviously must consider another question in connection with this subject, namely, Who can work miracles? This is a telling question when we remember that in Scripture, miracles were worked by God, Christ, servants of God at God's command, prophets, apostles, and other valid representatives of God. There is no question as to the validity of miracles by individuals specifically chosen of God and certified by Scripture.

But let us not forget the darker side of the picture. Miracles are also worked by Satan and his servants. Signs and wonders were worked by sorcerers and evil spirits (Exodus 7:11; 8:7; Matthew 24:24). According to Scripture, Satan himself is able to work miracles, and he will (Revelation 13:14; 16:14; 19:20).

The Antichrist will, after the working of Satan, be able to produce power, signs, and lying wonders (2 Thessalonians 2:9). Many other false servants will claim to have worked miracles. Those who hope to enter heaven one day will say to Christ, "Lord, . . . in thy name have [we not] cast out demons? And in thy name done many wonderful works?" (Matthew 7:22, NSRB). Christ's answer makes it clear that despite this supernatural ability, they were neither Christians nor servants of God. Although miracles are a supernatural working, that supernatural ability may come from a satanic source. Because of this, we are clearly admonished in Scripture to "try the spirits" (1 John 4:1).

We cannot emphasize this too greatly: all spiritual activity is not necessarily produced by our heavenly Father. Satan does indeed work miracles. He does this to add credence to his false doctrines. Because of this clever activity by our satanic adversary, we should be most careful and fearful of too easily believing and too quickly rejoicing in the reports from here and there of supernatural phenomena.

"But," we may argue, "is there not a legitimate place for believing God for a miracle within the activity of Chris-

tians?" This raises a fourth question. Will faith produce
miracles? Many claim, based on the promises of Christ,
that proper faith will produce a miraculous working of
God. Much modern preaching claims that strong faith will
produce great miracles and that weak faith will produce
small miracles, but that the miraculous is available to us
all as a result of our faith. The great chapter on faith will
help us in this regard.

Hebrews 11 tells us of some remarkable results that
faith produced in the lives of people. We may be astonished to note that almost all of these results are inner attitudes and external human activities as against miraculous
workings of God. In Hebrews 11, faith produces understanding (v. 3), the ability to make an offering (v. 4), the
diligence to prepare an ark (v. 7), obedience (v. 8), and
strength (v. 11). It produced in Isaac the ability to bless
Jacob (v. 20); in Jacob, the ability to bless both of Joseph's
sons and to worship God (v. 21). By faith, Joseph "made
mention of the departing of the children of Israel" (v. 22).

By faith, Moses was hidden (v. 23). Also by faith, Moses "refused" (v. 24), he "forsook" (v. 27), he "kept" (v.
28). By faith, the children of Israel "passed through the
Red Sea" (v. 29). Precious few of the results of faith in Hebrews 11 could come under the heading of overt miracles.
Most of the results of faith were inner resolution by which
individuals believed God and patiently labored for Him.
The list of the heroes of faith from verse 32 to verse 40 includes only a few miracles, but the larger result of faith
was the ability to endure cruel afflictions and even to die
without seeing the results of one's faith or receiving the
promise.

The apparent message of Hebrews 11 was that those
who had faith were able to go through painful experiences
and did not need a miracle to sustain them. This is consistent with the great statement of faith made by Job in the
midst of his grievous difficulties. Looking into the face of

his God, he said, "Though he slay me, yet will I trust in him" (Job 13:15).

A related question is, Do not miracles produce faith? The gospels' answer is no, not always. Thousands of individuals saw firsthand the miracles of Jesus Christ, beholding His divine and therefore remarkable ability to produce supernatural phenomena before their astonished eyes. We find, however, at the end of His earthly ministry, the multitudes rejected Him as their Messiah and hated Him for those very divine qualities.

The miracles of Christ had little permanent impact upon most of those who saw them. His miracles did not create living faith by which they would follow Him. An illustration of the inability of miracles to produce faith themselves is in Matthew 16:8-10. "Which when Jesus perceived, he said unto them, O ye of little faith, why reason ye among yourselves, because ye have brought no bread? Do ye not yet understand, neither remember the five loaves of the five thousand, and how many baskets ye took up? Neither the seven loaves of the four thousand, and how many baskets ye took up?" Christ indicts His hearers, because, though they saw the miracles, they neither believed nor understood Him or the nature of His ministry. Faith is produced, not by miracles, but by a knowledge of the Bible. "Faith cometh by hearing, and hearing by the word of God" (Romans 10:17). An understanding of Christian doctrine will produce faith within the heart, and no external phenomenon, apart from this understanding, will cause us to believe.

A further question regarding miracles is, Do faithful, spiritual people really need to see a sign or a miracle? Nothing is clearer from the earthly ministry of Christ than that those who were constantly asking for a miracle and a sign were those whose hearts were furthest from Him. They were the unbelieving, and often, they were the critics and the hecklers. Those who lived in the quiet confidence that Jesus Christ was the Son of God were happy to listen with loving contentment to His words and lessons for them.

The other group, those who cared nothing for the real Jesus Christ or the real salvation that He had to offer, were the object of the scathing denunciation of Christ, "A wicked and adulterous generation seeketh after a sign; and there shall no sign be given unto it, but the sign of the prophet Jonas. And he left them, and departed" (Matthew 16:4). These forceful words of our Savior should give us a better understanding of those who seek miracles, demand signs, put out fleeces, and give themselves to other similar insults to God. The call for a miracle characterized the carnal and unbelieving, not the spiritual.

Because we are concerned, we must continue to question. The questions that logically follow are, Will not God work a miracle in answer to a given prayer? What is the formula for scriptural prayer?

A partial list of those qualities of prayer which will enable us to pray in a scriptural fashion would be most instructive.

1. We must pray in the name of Christ. "Whatsoever ye shall ask in my name, that will I do, that the Father may be glorified in the Son" (John 14:13).
2. We must ask in faith. "Let him ask in faith, nothing wavering" (James 1:6).
3. We must be abiding in Christ. "If ye abide in me, and my words abide in you, ye shall ask what ye will, and it shall be done unto you" (John 15:7).
4. We must have His Word abiding in us (John 15:7).
5. We must not pray selfishly. "Ye ask, and receive not, because ye ask amiss, that ye may consume it upon your lusts" (James 4:3).
6. We must not waver in our faith. "But let him ask in faith, nothing wavering. For he that wavereth is like a

wave of the sea driven with the wind and tossed " (James 1:6-7).

7. We must not harbor known sin. "If I regard iniquity in my heart, the Lord will not hear me" (Psalm 66:18).

8. We must pray that the Father may be glorified (John 14:13).

9. We must be continuing in our prayers. "Continue in prayer, and watch in the same with thanksgiving" (Colossians 4:2).

10. We must give things time to work together for good. "We know that all things work together for good to them that love God, to them who are the called according to his purpose" (Romans 8:28).

11. We must remember that we reap in due season. "Let us not be weary in well doing: for in due season we shall reap, if we faint not" (Galatians 6:9).

12. We must finally resign ourselves to the will of God. As Christ said, "Nevertheless not as I will, but as thou wilt" (Matthew 26:39).

13. We must remember that the will of God is not always known to us. "For as the heavens are higher than the earth, so are my ways higher than your ways, and my thoughts than your thoughts" (Isaiah 55:9). "For who hath known the mind of the Lord? or who hath been his counsellor?" (Romans 11:34).

These characteristics of prevailing prayer are not to discourage us but to warn us against spiritual presumption. God gives us these modifiers that will keep us from going off the deep end as we seek the Lord for answers.

These scriptural principles also serve to remind us to reject the human formulas for prayer by those who promote "miraculous" answers. Clever spiritual formulas are commonly advocated by those who hold to some sort of automatic *A-B-C*-type prayer involvement with God. The formulas are many, but most of them boil down to a three-stage approach. One, have faith; two, send me your prayer request and believe in "my prayers"; three, make a contribution to my cause. These religious charlatans ought to be held in sustained contempt by all spiritual and reasonable people. We have seen that the satanic doctrine is almost true, that "all that a man hath will he give for his life." This almost truth has enriched the professional miracleworkers to an astonishing and heartbreaking degree.

How then shall we pray? The answer to that is clear from the life and experience of the apostle Paul. Paul had a painful affliction, a "thorn in the flesh." Understandably, he prayed that he might be delivered from it. He prayed not once, but three times. The answer that the Lord gave to him is fraught with spiritual lessons that would be of value for each of us. His loving Lord responded to his prayers by saying, "My grace is sufficient for thee: for my strength is made perfect in weakness" (2 Corinthians 12:9).

Paul, understanding this gracious response of his heavenly Father, gratefully declared, "Most gladly therefore will I rather glory in my infirmities, that the power of Christ may rest upon me. Therefore I take pleasure in infirmities, in reproaches, in necessities, in persecutions, in distresses for Christ's sake: for when I am weak, then am I strong" (2 Corinthians 12:9-10). How shall we pray? We should pray with an attitude that leaves the results with God and rejoices in them. For the believer, nothing is better than sufficient grace.

What then do we understand about miracles? A divine miracle is a working of God in contrast to the normal laws of nature, the exercise of which depends finally on His own sovereignty. He invites us to pray, to have faith in Him, and to trust Him for His best. The method of God's response to that faith and trust must obviously be left in His hands. There is a time to live and a time to die. There is a time to be sick and a time to be well, and all of these states can be endured to the glory of God.

Then let us ask that one final question. Is a miracle

God's modus operandi? Is a miracle the normal way God intends to work with us, and is it true that if we had more faith, we would see miracles as a regular practice? The answer is no. Here is why.

The devil was in effect saying, "Circumvent natural law in favor of a miracle," when he told Christ to command that the stones turn into bread.

How are we supposed to get bread? The normal way is that wheat is grown in the field, brought to the granary, ground into flour, and baked into loaves. In the process, many people are given gainful employment, and the final consumer of the bread appreciates both the blessing of God and the labor of man. The modus operandi of God, then, is not miracles; it is natural law.

If God is to work a miracle, He must do it only occasionally. For God to reach into the natural universe and work in contrast to the operation of the universe may well disturb the balance of nature beyond repair. God may make it rain upon occasion, but He must not do this too often because He has promised never to flood the world again. It is true that God supplied the needs of some people by a method that occasionally appears to be miraculous, but He must not do this too often because soon even Christians will become spiritually irresponsible as they did at the church at Thessalonica. Some turned into busybodies, "working not at all" (2 Thessalonians 3:11), and were charity cases under the welfare program of the church. Therefore, the rule was, "If any would not work, neither should he eat" (2 Thessalonians 3:10). They were to be fed not by a miracle but by their responsible labor.

Shall we then learn to *expect* miracles? Surely, we have no scriptural warrant for so doing. We must rather remember that "whatsoever a man soweth, that shall he also reap. For he that soweth to his flesh shall of the flesh reap corruption; but he that soweth to the Spirit shall of the Spirit reap life everlasting" (Galatians 6:7-8). This is the path to spiritual responsibility.

Many efforts for God are produced across the world by people who labor, suffer affliction, hunger, and endure persecution. In this, they assemble the human components of a mighty work for God. God in His love does *not* choose to do the whole work Himself, for "we are labourers together with God" (1 Corinthians 3:9). God has not offered Himself to us as a magician, but rather as the Savior, both of our souls and of our competence. Competent, spiritual people will take God at His word and endeavor to be effective, responsible workers together with Him. They will not accept Satan's lie that God is waiting at our beck and call for miracles on demand.

9

"Exploit the Promises"

The most remarkable book that has ever appeared on the human scene is the Bible. Written over the course of 1,500 years by more than forty authors, it claims and demonstrates that it is more than the words of eloquent men. It is indeed the very Word of the living God. When the believer says, "I rest upon Your Word alone," he claims the surest foundation available to man in this unsure world. He has stepped upon a rock that cannot be shaken, by believing in the Scripture that cannot be broken.

One of the reasons Scripture is a source of solace in time of sorrow and strength in time of weakness is the sure promises it contains. Peter said,

> According as his divine power hath given unto us all things that pertain unto life and godliness, through the knowledge of him that hath called us to glory and virtue: whereby are given unto us exceeding great and precious promises: that by these ye might be partakers of the divine nature, having escaped the corruption that is in the world through lust. (2 Peter 1:3-4)

Exceeding great and precious promises! God has indeed made several thousand promises to various people at various times, and not one of these promises has failed or will fail. Men of God throughout the ages have done remarkable feats because they believed the Word of God and were convinced that the promises of God were absolutely trustworthy. One of these was Abraham, who "staggered not at the promises of God through unbelief; but was strong in faith, giving glory to God; and being fully persuaded that, what he had promised, he was able also to perform. And therefore it was imputed to him for righteousness" (Romans 4:20-22).

Abraham believed God (literally, he said amen to God), and this became the basis for the gift of righteousness that he received from the Lord.

The stories of Abraham and other heroes of faith were not written simply to tell fascinating stories but that we might read and be encouraged in our faith. So, Paul says about Abraham, "Now it was not written for his sake alone, that it was imputed to him; but for us also, to whom it shall be imputed, if we believe on him that raised up Jesus our Lord from the dead; who was delivered for our offenses, and was raised again for our justification" (Romans 4:23-25).

We who are Christians can say with Solomon that God has not failed one word of His promise (1 Kings 8:56). With joy, we have sung,

> Standing on the promises that cannot fail,
> When the howling storms of doubt and fear assail.
> By the living word of God I shall prevail,
> Standing on the promises of God.

Any Christian will be greatly encouraged when he studies the Word of God and lists for his own soul's satisfaction the promises of God.

But there is a danger here. Danger, because Satan's next doctrine has to do with a presumptuous relationship to the promises of God. The eighth doctrine of the devil is, "Exploit the promises."

We learn of this doctrine from a further statement by Satan during the temptation of Christ.

What a scene that must have been! "Then the devil taketh him up into the holy city, and setteth him on a pinnacle of the temple" (Matthew 4:5). Satan and Christ were now looking down upon the multitudes who gathered in the Temple courtyard, assembling for worship. Possibly, thousands were in the Temple area on that occasion. Furthermore, they were in a religious state of mind and probably would have been deeply impressed if a major miracle had been performed in their presence on such an occasion. It is also entirely likely that the performer of this miracle would have impressed a multitude of people to believe in his divine abilities and thereby gained their following. The religious promoter would think very deeply as to how to exploit such a moment of opportunity!

With this in mind, listen to the words that Satan now speaks to Christ. "If thou be the Son of God, cast thyself down: for it is written, He shall give his angels charge concerning thee: and in their hands they shall bear thee up, lest at any time thou dash thy foot against a stone" (Matthew 4:6).

Again, we see our enemy moving in most subtle fashion, producing temptation on the highest spiritual plane. He invites Christ to produce a spiritual spectacular, and he quotes—actually misquotes—the Word of God to enhance that temptation. He attempts to entice Christ to exploit the promises of God.

What of this promise of Scripture? Is it valid? Certainly it is. One of the most blessed psalms is Psalm 91, in which David promises the protection and help of God to his own despite impossible external circumstances. This wonderful psalm has been a source of solace to believers in all of the ages. Who of us does not rejoice today in the many occasions in which we have seen these promises of protection and help abundantly fulfilled?

To this passage, the devil turns when he would corrupt the spiritual life of our Savior. He quotes a valid promise from God, not merely a piece of philosophic reasoning. It is not impossible that Satan expanded on this, reminding the Lord of the spectacular results that could come from such an exploit as jumping off the Temple but landing safely on the pavement below. Surely, thousands would be impressed with this magnificent feat, and they would turn from their lesser pursuits to follow Him.

In the same fashion, Satan appeals to would-be spiritual leaders of our present world, tempting them to move in the realm of the spectacular. Just as he invited Jesus Christ to become a superstar, he tempts men today to resort to one form of magic or another. He suggests that this is the key to success. He awakens the hope of making a lasting impression on people, obscuring the fact that the spectacular, even if successful, only impresses superficially, the response lasting no longer than other fascinations; and soon, the people are calling for better, more spectacular tricks from greater magicians.

But has not Satan in a great measure succeeded in his call to spiritual presumption? How many are those in places of religious influence today who have forsaken piety for public relations? Promotion has become king, even in the work of the Lord. Large segments of the church have ceased to believe in the power of prevailing prayer and have expanded their dependence on the power of hidden persuaders. We remind ourselves that the biggest men in popular religion today hire public relations firms and ad men to tailor their image for the newspapers and television sets of waiting and impressionable multitudes.

There is no question that a promotional program can be a vital instrument in the hands of God in producing a spiritual impact. But, is a person's large promotional program the *cause* of his apparent spiritual success, or has he not had spiritual success first and his expanded influence is the result of the blessing of God upon an honest and faithful life? The first kind of promotion results in failure, whereas the second is the outward expression of success in the inner man. So it is that "promotion cometh neither from the east, nor from the west, nor from the south. But God . . . putteth down one, and setteth up another" (Psalm 75:6).

The name of Jesus Christ is famous today "from Greenland's icy mountains to India's coral strand." This fame, however, is not because He cast Himself off the Temple. It is because He eschewed such insanities and gave Himself to fulfill the purpose of God for His life in going to the cross and dying for the sins of the world.

The best answer to Satan's suggestion of exploiting God's promises for the sake of sensationalism is also an important point of sound Christian doctrine. In response to Satan's invitation, Jesus commands, "Thou shalt not put the Lord thy God to the test" (Matthew 4:7, NSRB).

The devil invites each of us to take the initiative and exploit the promises of God. Conversely, Jesus Christ warns us that we are forbidden to put God to the test. Tempting God, or putting Him to the test, is doing the devil's work. It is in opposition to the promised method of the working of God. We cannot sue God. We must not "bring Him to court" to produce what we presume He has promised. To bring a delinquent God to the dock and demand our rights as if He were some heavenly deadbeat is a grievous sin.

There are many ways in which this can be attempted, some of which are explained in the New Testament. We have the promise that "God shall supply all your need according to his riches in glory by Christ Jesus" (Philippians 4:19). Some people would hold that this is a promise that God will take care of us no matter how lazy or irresponsible we are.

Even Paul, who recorded this promise, worked as a

tentmaker to support himself so that he would not be chargeable to any of the churches to whom he preached. He said, "These hands have ministered to my necessities, and to them that were with me" (Acts 20:34). The New Testament is filled with calls to diligence and carefulness lest Christians get the reputation of being fools whose foolishness is based on a false view of Scripture. Thou shalt not tempt the Lord thy God!

Paul states the basis of the Christian life when he says, "The just shall live by faith" (Romans 1:17), meaning, of course, faith in Christ for salvation. After salvation, it means to conduct ourselves according to the instructions and commandments of Scripture, living a disciplined and productive Christian life. To live by faith means to develop one's life in allegiance to the whole counsel of God.

By contrast there are those who announce that they are "living by faith," meaning that they do nothing to support themselves or the work of Christ. They become charity cases, adding to the bad reputation that the church already has in some places for spiritual foolishness. In their case, living life by faith becomes an excuse for laziness or incompetence. They presume that their need will be supplied no matter how irresponsibly they live. You shall not put the Lord your God to the test!

It is Satan who tempts us to perform a dangerous "act of faith," thereby forcing God to work a miracle to save us. In the face of this insane call, we have the absolute command of Christ. "Thou shalt not put the Lord thy God to the test." Who are we to force the God of the universe to do anything?

The prohibition against testing God is found in many places in Scripture. The children of Israel sinned because they put God to the test (Exodus 17:2). The Corinthian church was reminded of this occasion lest they become foolish in this same fashion (1 Corinthians 10:9). This is especially significant when we remember that the Corinthians were famous phenomenalists, who believed that faith must produce some spectacular events to prove itself. This carnal and corrupt church, in violation of the Word of God, gave itself to the foolish pursuit of phenomena rather than the studied development of mature faith.

We all should rethink what we mean when we say that we are standing on the promises of God. If we are resting in the Lord as the source of our ultimate confidence, holding that the will of God will finally be done, whether we see it or not, well and good. If, however, we are tempted to exploit the promises of God in the name of our "deeply spiritual" faith, we may find ourselves doing the devil's work to the damage of our own souls and to the hurt of the faith of those who look to us for an example. We have already seen that God has ordained natural law and it is on the basis of natural law that He normally intends to work in our lives. Whether or not we see a miracle is entirely up to God. Miracle on demand is never given to us as a method of operation in doing the work of God.

Make no mistake about it, if we would master another language, we must study. If we would have a church building, we must build it. If we would preach and teach well, we must learn the Word of God. The same God who wrote the Scripture ordained that the law of gravity would operate on all normal occasions. The Christian, no matter how spiritual he pretends to be, is a fool if he expects that God will cancel that law in his favor whenever he chooses or pleases.

Why is it that God tells us never to put Him to the test? The reasons are obvious. The first is that we may have the wrong understanding of the promise. For instance, when we read the promise, "My God shall supply all your need," we may really have little idea as to what our real need is. We may tell ourselves that we need great riches when our real need may be severe discipline. We may think our most pressing need is the love of this man or that woman, but we may be asking for a hell on earth.

Our understanding about ourselves and about God is limited enough so that we should be careful about prescribing to God how He shall fulfill this promise to us. Only omniscience knows the exact nature of our *real* need.

A second reason we must be careful about putting God to the test is that we may be attempting to claim a promise that simply does not apply to us at all. For instance, how often have we quoted in our churches 2 Chronicles 7:14, "If my people, which are called by my name, shall humble themselves, and pray, and seek my face, and turn from their wicked ways; then will I hear from heaven, and will forgive their sin, and will heal their land?" Christians of many nations have prayed on the basis of this verse that "their land" would be healed, forgiven, and saved. The fact is that this promise was given to the nation of Israel and has not been repeated for the benefit of the British, the Americans, or the Koreans. Now, surely, God will bring blessing to any land that is the object of the ministry of faithful Christians, but the promise of 2 Chronicles 7:14 simply cannot be invoked for a modern nation in the same sense that it was given to the Jews.

Christians are frequently encouraged to become tithers on the basis of the promise of Malachi 3:10. "Bring ye all the tithes into the storehouse, that there may be meat in mine house, and prove me now herewith, saith the Lord of hosts, if I will not open you the windows of heaven, and pour you out a blessing, that there shall not be room enough to receive it." This surely was a wonderful promise made to the nation of Israel, that the tithing of the people of God would be the *cause* for the prosperity that God would minister to them in return. He would pour them out a blessing greater than they could receive.

Does this also apply to Christians? Each Christian is called to give as God has prospered. The argument is very sound that if one tithed under the law, surely he should give much more than this under grace. To argue, however,

that tithing is the basis of the blessing of God in our lives
in the same sense that it was in the Old Testament, is a
misapplication of the promise of God. Every Christian is
blessed with all spiritual blessings in heavenly places in
Christ (Ephesians 1:3). This is not because he tithes, or
works, or does anything else to earn it. This is because of
the grace of Jesus Christ and becomes the portion of the
Christian because of the finished work of Calvary. Our
working for God, our giving, and our faithful service in no
way *cause* the blessing of God, but rather these are our
grateful responses to spiritual blessings we have already
received in Jesus Christ. In this case of misapplication, a
promise becomes a limiting factor rather than a source of
spiritual encouragement.

A further reason we must be careful about putting
God to the test is that we may not be in a condition to receive God's promise. We remember that David said, "If I
regard iniquity in my heart, the Lord will not hear me."
The person who is not saved, or the Christian who is allowing a sinful condition to continue in his life, is in no
position to receive a promise of God except the promise of
judgment.

One of the great qualities of discernment that we
must be given of God is the ability to tell the difference
between faith and presumption. Faith has been the basis
upon which God has produced marvelous results in the
lives of believing people. Presumption, on the other hand,
has produced nothing but spiritual disaster. The fine line
between faith and presumption is obscure to many people. This obscurity, of course, is due to a lack of knowledge of the Word of God and therefore a deficiency of the
spiritual discernment which such knowledge produces.
Faith is a wonderful gift from God, but presumption is one
of Satan's most widely distributed products.

The question of course remains, How do we relate to
the promises of God? Is there any way that they can be
truly appropriated and made relevant and valuable in our

lives? The following are some simple rules for relating to the promises of God.

1. *The promises of God must not become a substitute for faithfulness.* The promise that all things are yours (1 Corinthians 3:22) or that God will give us "all things" (Romans 8:32) must never lead a person to become a thief under the argument that all things belong to him anyway. The Christian must work to support himself and his family, give to the work of God, study the Word, and be industrious in many other ways, despite the promise of God that the world belongs to us.

2. *Our interpretation of the promise must be consistent with the whole of Scripture.* We are promised in Psalm 91, "With long life will I satisfy him." Nevertheless, the Bible announces that the normal life of an individual will be "threescore years and ten" (Psalm 90:10). Therefore, one cannot reasonably pray that he will live to the age of two hundred.

3. *Our faith must not violate moral principles.* God has told us, "Whatsoever a man soweth, that shall he also reap" (Galatians 6:7). The principle applies to the chain smoker who prays that he will recover from thirty years of nicotine damage in a moment of miracle. In many ways, God has promised to deliver us, but Paul clearly said that if he had done anything "worthy of death," he refused "not to die" (Acts 25:11). He was conscious that he must not violate the moral cause and effect relationship on which the universe is built.

4. *We must remember that God may have a greater plan in mind.* It is possible that when Paul was being beaten with stripes in the city of Philippi and then thrown into prison, he might well have prayed that he would be instantly delivered from this situation. Instead, of course,

he rejoiced with Silas in their circumstances (Acts 16:25), for he sensed that God was working out a greater plan than that he be relieved at that moment from physical pain. The greater plan, of course, was the conversion of the Philippian jailer, which was the result of Paul's faith, indeed, even of his unwillingness to escape the prison. Some of us might have considered the open prison doors a miraculous deliverance.

Any of us would be a fool to forget that God may have a plan that is greater than our physical deliverance from distressing circumstances. He may even have a plan that is more important than our survival in a given circumstance. Surely the martyrdom of Stephen, who was not delivered from death, became a stirring example to his fellow Christians. There is much modern preaching that seems to forget that the Bible promises Christians, "Yea, and all that will live godly in Christ Jesus shall suffer persecution" (2 Timothy 3:12). "Unto you it is given in the behalf of Christ, not only to believe on him, but also to suffer for his sake" (Philippians 1:29). "They shall put you out of the synagogues: yea, the time cometh, that whosoever killeth you will think that he doeth God service" (John 16:2). "For they shall deliver you up to councils; and in the synagogues ye shall be beaten: and ye shall be brought before rulers and kings for my sake, for a testimony against them" (Mark 13:9). It is irresponsible to preach and foolish to believe that the will of God is always our instant satisfaction and our total pleasure and fulfillment *now.*

5. *We must not let the promises of God obscure the Person of God.* Surely, the greatest promise that Christ makes to any of us is, "I will never leave thee, nor forsake thee" (Hebrews 13:5). If my blessed Lord is with me in every circumstance of life, what else really matters? What bauble, what pleasure, what answer to a fearful prayer can compare with His personal presence with me today? We

have learned from the satanic discussion concerning Job that the devil would have us revere the blessings of God more than the God who gives those blessings. To lose sight of the Person because our eyes are filled with His gifts is to become a servant of Satan.

A. B. Simpson, founder of the Christian and Missionary Alliance, stated this spiritual principle perceptively:

> Once it was the blessing, now it is the Lord;
> Once it was the feeling, now it is His Word;
> Once His gift I wanted, now the Giver own;
> Once I sought for healing, now Himself alone,
>
> Once 'twas painful trying, now 'tis perfect trust;
> Once a half salvation, now the uttermost!
> Once 'twas ceaseless holding, now He holds me
> fast;
> Once 'twas constant drifting, now my anchor's
> cast.
>
> Once 'twas busy planning, now 'tis trustful
> prayer;
> Once 'twas anxious caring, now He has the
> care;
> Once 'twas what I wanted, now what Jesus says;
> Once 'twas constant asking, now 'tis ceaseless
> praise.
>
> Once it was my working, His it hence shall be;
> Once I tried to use Him, now He uses me;
> Once the power I wanted, now the Mighty One;
> Once for self I labored, now for Him alone.
>
> Once I hoped in Jesus, now I know He's mine;
> Once my lamps were dying, now they brightly
> shine;
> Once for death I waited, now His coming hail;
> And my hopes are anchored safe within the
> veil.

Well said. Mr. Simpson has given us eloquent testimony of the path toward spiritual maturity that he followed. His immature faith wanted the things of God. His mature faith then sought for only the Lord Himself.

There is a final question that we must face, and that is, Why do we have the promises of God? The answer may be best expressed in the form of an illustration. Outside of our cities, there are highways with sharp curves, bridges, and sometimes deep precipices. In these places, the highway department puts up a fence that, in effect, says, "Here is a promise; you will be protected from unusual danger at this point where the road curves." Now, what are we supposed to do with that promise? Shall we get a large truck, fill it full of heavy material, and drive it at a high speed into the retaining fence? Is this a good activity to "prove" whether the promising possibilities of the fence are true or not? The answer is that of course we should not. These retaining fences were placed there for a purpose, that is, to protect us from unusual circumstances.

If someone is driving along this road and suddenly a tire blows, he might be in great trouble. The car bounces against the retaining fence, returns to the road, and the damage is slight. But for the retaining fence, the driver and the automobile would have been in deep trouble. The fence and its implied promise became a source of deliverance.

This is something like the manner in which we are to relate to the promises of God. The normal course of events in our lives is that needs are supplied through work; health is sustained through diet, exercise, and even the help of a physician (as was the case with Paul). The extreme circumstances in life are rare. At that point, man's extremity may well become God's opportunity. The Lord may choose to avail Himself of this opportunity. Whether He does or does not, has nothing to do with His love or justice in the eyes of a trusting soul. It is, therefore, good to remind ourselves again of the imperative principle "The just shall live by faith."

10

"Satan's Way
Is the
Best Way"

Titanic forces are locked in combat for the rulership of the universe. When we realize that the world is being acted upon by an omnipotent God and a nearly omnipotent devil, we should be careful as to the placement of our loyalties. Each believer in Christ is thereby a protagonist in a spiritual struggle with stupendous issues. The kingdoms of this world, the moral balance of the universe, eternal life, and eternal death, all of these are at stake in the conflict of this age.

Because of this, the New Testament well advises us,

> Be strong in the Lord, and in the power of his might. Put on the whole armour of God, that ye may be able to stand against the wiles of the devil. For we wrestle not against flesh and blood, but against principalities, against powers, against the rulers of the darkness of this world, against spiritual wickedness in high places. Wherefore take unto you the whole armour of God, that ye may be able to withstand in the evil day, and having done all, to stand. (Ephesians 6:10-13)

We are further warned, "Be sober, be vigilant; because your adversary the devil, as a roaring lion, walketh about, seeking whom he may devour" (1 Peter 5:8). Again,

"Woe to the inhabiters of the earth and of the sea! For the devil is come down unto you, having great wrath, because he knoweth that he hath but a short time" (Revelation 12:12).

Our essential struggle is not one of guns and bombs, nor one that will be decided by the conquest of square miles of real estate. Rather, this conflict is resident in the moral universe, the physical world being one arena of that greater struggle. The presence of this spiritual conflict comes as a shock to some who have hoped that they might be allowed to live quiet and unperturbed lives. If our lives appear to be undisturbed, it is only because we are momentarily in the passing point of equal tensions in this fierce conflict. "In the world ye shall have tribulation" is more nearly the description of the status quo of our lives.

The critical time in that great conflict between Christ and Satan came in the last point of the temptation. In the preceding two attempts, Satan revealed additional points in his perverse doctrine. Having failed to corrupt the Son of God in these, he now moves closer to the line of desperation as he makes our Lord a final offer.

> Again, the devil taketh him up into an exceeding high mountain, and sheweth him all the kingdoms of the world, and the glory of them; And saith unto him, All these things will I give thee, if thou wilt fall down and worship me. Then saith Jesus unto him, Get thee hence, Satan: for it is written, Thou shalt worship the Lord thy God, and him only shalt thou serve. (Matthew 4:8-10)

Here is revealed the ninth doctrine of his infernal majesty, namely, "Satan's way is the best way."

This temptation is most stunning. Up until this point, no human had ever been presented with such an offer. Until now, the normal approach in satanic temptation had been to offer just a little bit. Satan takes fiendish glee in corrupting an eternal soul with as pitiful a temporal prize as possible. Eve gave in because of the offer of a bit of experiential knowledge and a few bites of a forbidden fruit. Esau sold out for a bowl of food to satisfy temporary hunger. Achan threw in the towel for a wedge of gold and a goodly Babylonish garment. David committed his great sin because of one erotic scene—Bathsheba at her bath.

This is the kind of bargain that Satan usually offers. He asks for nearly everything and in return gives almost nothing. He counts on the fact that the individual's sense of value is so distorted that he will pay and pay again for empty packages. We chase the will-o'-the-wisp of economic gain, corporate advancement, human applause, or personal satisfaction. We carry in our hand our divine birthright, thoughtlessly trading it for a mess of pottage. Satan wins easily and without a struggle with most of us.

With ridiculous ease, his infernal majesty, the devil, also subverts most of us by proxy. He rarely needs to appear on the scene, for he knows that he can trust the established pattern of our society to press upon us its lusts and sins in the name of status. The world and the flesh have served the cause of iniquity so successfully that Satan must be close to boredom with inactivity. Through centuries of nearly effortless conquest, our enemy has grown fat on the swill of little souls and easy subversions. The moral death that comes to most people is not murder by the devil but merely another case of voluntary spiritual suicide.

Thankfully, this was not the case with Jesus Christ. Satan's approach failed, for Christ would not work a miracle on demand for His own physical need. The spiritual presumption approach failed, for Christ would not exploit the promise of God foolishly. In this breathless moment, Satan now makes a final decision. Revealing his own deep spiritual inversion, he offers his own "birthright" for a moment's sincere respect by the Person who was the essence of moral purity—Jesus Christ the Son of God. In this utterly important moment, the moral balance of the world is at stake. Here, Satan sees that his opportunity to seduce Christ into sin is slipping away, and therefore he makes a desperate, last offer. He offers to Christ the kingdoms of this world.

We must not doubt that Satan was making a valid offer. When Adam sinned, the planet earth was conceded to the devil; Adam and his heirs lost their dominion to him. In Scripture, therefore, he is rightly called the prince of this world (John 14:30), the god of this world (2 Corinthians 4:4), and the prince of the power of the air (Ephesians 2:2). He is "the spirit that now worketh in the children of disobedience" (Ephesians 2:2), and therefore we are warned that "the whole world lieth in wickedness" (1 John 5:19). The world system is owned and operated by his infernal majesty, the devil, and now he offers it to Christ in return for His worship. Here is one of the most important moments in all of history.

The diabolical aspect of this temptation is that the offer of Satan was both true and false. It is presumably true that Satan would have given to Christ the kingdoms of this world. The false aspect of this temptation, however, was that Christ would have achieved this point of rulership only by conceding in advance to the ultimate rulership of Satan. He would not have ruled the kingdoms of this world in His own name but as a surrogate of the devil. An act of worship before his infernal majesty would have amounted to an eternal concession that Satan was the final ruler. No one can rule independently if his independence has already been taken from him. When one submits himself to satanic leadership, he becomes a slave to the devil.

We cannot know all of the Savior's thoughts, but we can be sure that He was pressed by the weight of temptation in its most attractive and potentially horrible form. We are informed that Christ was "in all points tempted like as we" (Hebrews 4:15). All of the pull of satanic magnetism was presented in its strongest form in the temptation of Christ.

From this encounter, we can know the method Christ used to withstand against the powerful pressure of Satan. Note again the words of our Savior, "Thou shalt worship the Lord thy God, and him only shalt thou serve." Christ involved Himself in no philosophic discussion about the nature of temptation, the validity of this satanic offer, or the economic value of the kingdoms of this world. He did not even ask for the opportunity to think it over. Not compromising, His response was instant, straightforward, and total. It was a clear, final no!

The fact that the worship of any thing or person beside God is forbidden in Scripture was enough for Jesus Christ. The law of God was the foundation for the spiritual conviction of the Lord Jesus.

The consequence of this righteous act is that the moral balance of the universe has not been overturned. Sin is still sin; righteousness is still righteousness. We can thank Jesus Christ and His reliance upon the law of God for this. It is wise, therefore, to bear in mind that the world is still under the unbroken moral law of God. No matter how rebellious men and nations may have become, God is still in control of His universe. The immortal words of Browning's "Epilogue to Asolando" are still true.

> Never doubted clouds would break,
> Never dreamed, though right were worsted,
> Wrong would triumph, held we fall to rise,
> Are baffled to fight better,
> Sleep to wake.

No matter how much evil seems to prosper, the ultimate base and the final reality of the universe is not evil; it is good.

As we have noted, in this last phase of the temptation, Satan reveals another of his doctrinal positions; the real way to gain the kingdoms of this world is to worship Satan; the path to progress, capability, and fulfillment is to turn from fidelity to the living God and commit our lives to the worship of the devil. We are asked to believe that Satan's way is the best way, that is, superior to the way of God. This view is completely anti-God.

And, as astonishing as it may seem, that view is gaining credence. The outright worship of Satan is increasingly popular among otherwise intelligent people. From major cities and rural areas across America and the Western world come frightening reports of individuals who have committed their lives to Satan and who have literally fallen down to worship him.

In our time, institutions, cultic religions, and movements that call for outright worship of Satan have formed in great numbers. They declare Lucifer the true king of the universe. I have personally seen pamphlets distributed to high school students in a Southern California city giving them detailed instructions on how to make a covenant with Lucifer. The material claims that Lucifer is the true god and advocates the blasphemy that Christ is a usurper. It tells the proper candles and incantations to use for the commitment of one's soul to Satan.

So it is that various forms of the occult have trapped many naive and irresponsible souls into a form of anti-God, anti-Christ religious activity. The evidence continues to mount that multiplied thousands are involving themselves in this aberrant, religious behavior. The prophetic Scriptures warn us of the time when the world will worship the Antichrist, the representative of the devil on earth.

So, the spiritist and witchcraft scene commits itself to anti-God religious worship with all its frightening implications. Thousands have stood on smaller mountains than the mount of Christ's temptation and looked on lesser kingdoms and have quickly said yes to Satan, where Christ said an emphatic no. The corrupt lives and blasted psyches of the hapless victims of today's dark, satanic practices are an illustration of the kind of awful fate that was spared us by the moral victory of Christ.

This satanic doctrine can also be expressed in another form, helping us to see its frightening application to larger multitudes of people. In this variant version, Satan has said, "There is a way to human achievement other than the worship of and fidelity to the true God." In this lesser form, this doctrine of the devil has corrupted more millions of people than many of us could possibly imagine. Since God is omnipotent, omniscient, and omnipresent, and since Jesus Christ is the Creator and Sustainer of all things, it follows that there is no morally correct alternative to doing the will of the true and living God.

To hold that any other entity in the universe has final value and therefore can legitimately be worshiped for its own intrinsic worth is idolatry. There is no final value in the universe other than God. God, by His very nature, must be exclusivistic. He confesses that He is "a jealous God." This, of course, is not a fault in His personality, but simply a true expression that he is the ultimate fact, the uncaused cause. All other values are derivative of His value, His ultimacy.

It follows, therefore, that the commitment of one's life to any value or object of worship that is less than God is ultimately a satanic commitment. Jesus Christ expressed this clearly by saying, "Thou shalt worship the Lord thy God, and Him *only* shalt thou serve" (emphasis added). There is no pluralism as to the rulership of the universe. All rulers derive their authority from the final rulership of God.

It follows, then, that the world's problems are so because of the unwillingness of men to admit to and submit to the final authority of the eternal God. The satanic doctrine of the supremacy or the worthiness of another entity beside the Lord has permeated the thinking of men to a frightening degree. The promotion of the worship of a god less than the true God is a practice indulged in by many of the rulers of this world and not a few of their followers.

The Greek mythologist created gods to fulfill all of the lesser functions. There was a god of war, a god of fertility, a god that produced prosperity, and so on, ad infinitum. The Roman world finally established thousands of gods, covering every real and imagined need. The result of commitment to any one of these gods was, of course, damnation, because the corollary to the supremacy of God is that all other gods must be satanic, ultimately producing damnation. For this reason, the children of Israel were commanded as a first principle of their law,

> Thou shalt have no other gods before me. Thou shalt not make unto thee any graven image, or any likeness of any thing that is in heaven above, or that is in the earth beneath, or that is in the water under the earth. Thou shalt not bow down thyself to them, nor serve them: for I the Lord thy God am a jealous God, visiting the iniquity of the fathers upon the children unto the third and fourth generation of them that hate me; and showing mercy unto thousands of them that love me, and keep my commandments. (Exodus 20:3-6)

This law is not some arbitrary municipal statute made by a local legislator. It is a simple necessity. If God is God, which He is, it could not be otherwise.

That truth has great implications for us. The Christian faith, by this world's standards, is a most exclusive, arrogant faith. Christianity claims for itself ultimate truth, and it insists that other propositional theologies are infinitely inferior to it. The Christian is to believe and serve no other truth and to admit to no other authority, in the sense of agreeing that that authority is final.

This concept of final truth enabled Christ to resist the offer of Satan. He took refuge, not in argument, but in the Word of God. Satan's offer was certainly most appealing, but it became utterly ridiculous in the light of the final truth of Scripture. Jesus Christ's confidence in the truth of the Word of God made it possible for Him to be justified

in His sayings and to overcome in this situation of temptation. He did not resist the devil by some rare form of spiritual activity. He did not involve Himself by using reason,
subtle theological argument, or even what we might call
earnest prayer. His method was to invoke the authority of
the Word of God. In each of the temptations, He quoted
Scripture and rested on the sure Word of God as it spoke
to the particular temptation. The lesson is clear. Each of
us, if we are to resist the horrible pressure of clever, satanic temptation, must resort to a knowledge greater than
our own. We must acquire a knowledge of the Word of
God, and we must invoke that knowledge at the point of
moral pressure. Knowing and using the Bible will be for us,
as it was for Christ, the source of spiritual strength that
can produce victory over temptation.

The promise of personal vindication and triumph is
utterly valid for us, if we follow the same commitment to
the Word of God as was true about Jesus Christ. There
may be a thousand versions of this satanic doctrine, some
of them so sophisticated as to be almost unanswerable,
but they all are belied when we answer them with the refutation of Scripture. There is, therefore, no better course
to recommend than a thoroughgoing, working knowledge
of the Bible. By this knowledge alone, we will be able to
withstand the wiles of the devil.

We must not doubt that Satan is constantly pressur-
ing us to recast our loyalties in some other direction beside the Person of Jesus Christ and His will for our lives.
We do well to review daily the commitments of our lives
and ask anew if a god has intervened in our worship of our
blessed Lord, turning us into sophisticated pagans. With
this knowledge, we can understand and repeat the prayer
of William Cowper:

> The dearest idol I have known,
> Whate'er that idol be,
> Help me to tear it from Thy throne
> And worship only Thee.

So shall my walk be close with God,
Calm and serene my frame;
So purer light shall mark the road
That leads me to the Lamb.

The spiritually perceptive soul is conscious that many idols are constantly attempting to creep onto the altar of worship of God. There are many external alternatives and inner attitudes that, with the help of Satan, can drive a wedge between us and our heavenly Father. In the face of these dreadful, satanic alternatives, we must heed the absolute command of Scripture, quoted by Jesus Christ: "Thou shalt worship the Lord thy God, and him only shalt thou serve."

11

"Don't Go
to the
Cross"

Life has a purpose. We are here in this world on a divine
mission. There is a reason for our existence, a reason that
is realizable in time and understandable in the light of
eternity. Unfortunately, this fact remains forever obscure
to most people. The lives of a majority of people, and most
would readily admit it, are without a personal goal. If it
ever occurs to them that life has a purpose, they quickly
escape from this nagging suspicion into a world of amuse-
ment or indulgence.

Life's purpose is given insufficient attention by most
of us. This inattention becomes tragic when we remember
that nothing in all of the world becomes useful or significant unless it functions in the fulfillment of its purpose.
The importance of purpose is so obvious that it is astonishing that we ignore this principle when considering the
greatest mission of all, life itself.

We can draw an inference from this disinterest in
life's purpose, namely, that when a person ignores the
purpose of life, he is not merely stupid, he is spiritually
subverted. He is being drawn into irrationality by a force
acting upon his thought processes, clouding his reason, so
that he does not see the foolishness of his position. As
Scripture warns, Satan himself is blinding his mind so that

the simple truth that life has a purpose continues to escape him.

We have already seen that one of the doctrines of the devil is to suggest that God has no true destiny for our lives. The final satanic doctrine that we shall consider is an expansion of this earlier suggestion. It is the call that says, "Don't give yourself to fulfill the purpose that God has for your life." Or, as he expressed it, in effect, "Don't go to the cross."

This satanic doctrine is revealed through a conversation between Christ and His disciples. As Christ approached the end of His three-year ministry, He began to introduce to His disciples the subject of His coming suffering and death on the cross. The possibility of the death of their beloved Leader was a prospect so foreign to the thinking of the disciples that they were hardly able to comprehend His presentation of this unspeakable fate. Was He not the Messiah? Did He not come to establish a great kingdom? Were not they, the disciples, to reign with Him in that kingdom? With these questions in mind, they could hardly endure the dark foreboding that grew in their minds as Christ talked about the future.

> time forth began Jesus to shew unto his disciples, how that he must go unto Jerusalem, and suffer many things of the elders and chief priests and scribes, and be killed, and be raised again the third day. Then Peter took him, and began to rebuke him, saying, Be it far from thee, Lord; this shall not be unto thee. But he turned, and said unto Peter, Get thee behind me, Satan: thou art an offense unto me: for thou savourest not the things that be of God, but those that be of men. (Matthew 16:21-23)

In this scene, Jesus announces that He is going to the cross, and Peter responds by saying, "Be it far from thee, Lord: this shall not be unto thee." Those who hold that Christ always spoke in gentle, saccharine, ambiguous words, are caught up short at His stern rebuke to Peter, "Get thee behind me, Satan." Our Lord was not detracted by Peter's statement, so expressive of "loving concern." He knew that the real author of the words of Peter was His old enemy, Satan. The enemy was active, even in that loving circle of Christ and His disciples, as they spoke together about the kingdom of God. In this intimate circle, Satan speaks, saying, "Don't go to the cross." Here, again, this tireless enemy of God attempts to deter the Lord Jesus Christ from fulfilling the purpose of His earthly life, to die for the sins of mankind and therefore provide redemption for a lost humanity.

Satan was well aware of this purpose. The plan of God for the coming and death of Jesus Christ had been announced many times in the Old Testament. Indeed, the first promise of redemption was given by God immediately following the Fall of man, which was Satan's first triumph over humanity. Speaking to the serpent, God had said, "And I will put enmity between thee and the woman, and between thy seed and her seed; it shall bruise thy head, and thou shalt bruise his heel" (Genesis 3:15). At all costs, Satan must not allow this plan for human redemption to be consummated in the death and resurrection of Jesus Christ. If, through the wonderful provision of God, man could be made a new creation, Satan's kingdom would be brought to ruin and his own doom sealed.

The record shows that Satan attempted in many ways to prevent God's program of redemption for a lost humanity. Consider some of these ways.

When the human race was corrupted by satanic activity in the sixth chapter of Genesis, the very survival of true humanity was at stake. The response of God was at once a loving and a destructive act. He sent the Flood and destroyed all human life except those eight souls that were aboard the ark. Had Satan succeeded in corrupting humanity in total, it would have been impossible for a human Savior to appear. Consequently, the promise that

Christ would be "the seed of a woman" would have been made impossible and thereby human salvation would have become impossible as well. This necessitated the purging of the human race, leaving eight uncorrupted people to repopulate the earth.

In another attempt to prevent redemption, Satan tried to destroy the Jewish race. This attempt is recounted for us in the magnificent book of Esther. Here, Israel in captivity is the object of a murderous conspiracy promoted by Haman, the chief minister of King Ahasuerus. Subverted by Haman's lies, Ahasuerus issued an edict that the Jews were to be destroyed and their property taken for spoil.

In this edict lay not only the fate of Israel but the fate of the human race. God had promised that He would send a divine Redeemer. This Redeemer would come out of Israel and would be of the tribe and lineage of David. Were Israel to be destroyed, this promise could not be fulfilled.

Happily, Haman's plan to destroy the Jews did not succeed. This was made possible in part because of the intervention of Esther, who was a Jew and the favorite queen of Ahasuerus. She persuaded her husband to allow the Jews to defend themselves, therefore surviving to beget Christ, the Author of the world's redemption.

In one of his bloodiest assaults, Satan continued in his plan to thwart divine redemption by attempting to kill Christ as a child. "Then Herod, when he saw that he was mocked of the wise men, was exceeding wroth, and sent forth, and slew all the children that were in Bethlehem, and in all the coasts thereof, from two years old and under, according to the time which he had diligently enquired of the wise men" (Matthew 2:16). So utterly shameless is this infant massacre that we can draw a conclusion about satanic effort. He will stop at nothing to destroy the purpose of God in the lives of people. He is without pity, implacable, unmerciful. It is nothing to him if the world runs red with blood, if only he can tear God from His throne. He is cruel beyond belief!

Now, on the occasion of Peter's statement, we find Satan making one of his last efforts to prevent human redemption. In the loving words of this earnest disciple, Satan implores Christ, "Don't go to the cross."

From Christ's response to these tempting words, we learn another lesson as to the method of the Lord Jesus in dealing with the devil. On each occasion where Satan obviously spoke to Jesus, he was immediately and totally repudiated by the Lord. Christ did not take the time to think about it, to ponder these words. He did not say, "Well, I'll sleep on it." Not for one moment did Christ give place to the devil by holding that his evil suggestions were worthy of intelligent consideration. Instantly and emphatically, He responds by saying, "Get thee behind me, Satan." This was not the time for sweet diplomacy with Satan or his spokesman. "Thou art an offense unto me" is a flat denunciation of both the devil and Peter, his temporary servant. No suggestions about friendship or inoffensiveness would have been wise here. The issue is clear, and Satan must be denounced. In this instant and total repudiation of Satan we see one of the reasons his temptation of Christ did not succeed: Christ was determined to go to the cross and fulfill the will of His Father.

We see many expressions of this utter purposefulness in the words of the Savior spoken in many places and in various circumstances. "I must work the works of him that sent me, while it is day" (John 9:4). When referring to the will of His Father, our Lord Jesus knew the meaning of the word *must*. His values made His life a living illustration of what He admonished everyone else to do. "Seek ye first the kingdom of God and his righteousness." First the will of God, first the fulfillment of life's purpose, first and foremost that eternal reason for which I am—these were the propositions that oriented the direction of Christ. This determination to fulfill the will of God is what made satanic temptation a resistible thing.

The result was that Jesus Christ did go to the cross and died to provide redemption for a lost mankind. His death wrought the final and most severe damage to Satan and to his kingdom. Through His death, Christ destroyed the works of the devil (1 John 3:8). He destroyed "him that had the power of death, that is, the devil" (Hebrews 2:14-15). His statement was utterly true that He made shortly before His crucifixion, "The prince of this world is judged" (John 16:11). On the cross, Genesis 3:15 is fulfilled. Here, the Seed of the woman has bruised the head of the serpent. One of the great testimonies of the defeat of Satan and his kingdom is in the announcement of the apostle Paul, "Therefore if any man be in Christ, he is a new creature: old things are passed away; behold, all things are become new" (2 Corinthians 5:17).

Never again can Satan come before Christ and offer Him the kingdoms of this world, for they are no longer his. Christ has redeemed them as His inheritance through His death upon the cross. In that all of these belong to Christ, the New Testament Christian is given a most wonderful promise, "He that spared not his own Son, but delivered him up for us all, how shall he not with him also freely give us all things?" (Romans 8:32). The reconquest of the moral universe by the captain of our salvation makes it possible for Paul to announce to Christians, "For all things are yours; whether Paul, or Apollos, or Cephas, or the world, or life, or death, or things present, or things to come; all are yours; and ye are Christ's; and Christ is God's" (1 Corinthians 3:21-23). How unutterably wonderful are the results of Christ's repudiation of the satanic doctrine, "Don't live up to the purpose of your life; don't go to the cross."

The results in the life of the person who believes in Jesus Christ will be correspondingly great. However, we may be sure that Satan will come to every one of us and preach the same destructive doctrine of self-preservation. In many ways, he will say, "Don't be a fool. Don't give yourself to so ridiculous a course as the denial of yourself in order to accomplish some abstract spiritual purpose. Accomplishment is here and now. It is made out of money, material, cars, homes, and human applause. This is the only world we know anything about, and any man is a fool to live for the world to come. Enjoy yourself. Live it up." With these and many other propositions, Satan continues to play the hackneyed record that one is a fool to live for any moment beyond the existential now. He has not been without real help in promoting that theme. From the old atheistic philosophers to the modern television writers, Satan's media representatives in almost every field have denied the existence of spiritual value or eternal purpose in life and avidly promoted that soul-destroying message. As a result, the theme of our generation is, "Live now; it's later than you think."

As a fearful consequence ,millions of people are turning aside from God's call and into the byways of this moment's indulgence. The man who dedicates himself to any cause that demands sacrifices, even on a human level, is accounted a fool by most people. Especially is the Christian accounted a fool. The young person who turns his back upon public applause and big money to give himself to the service of God is laughed at, sometimes even by his fellow Christians. The experience of each servant of God assures us that Satan will predictably find a way to say to us, "Don't give yourself to the point of death for a divine reason; don't be a fool."

We have, by contrast, the invitation of Jesus Christ: "If any man will come after me, let him deny himself, and take up his cross, and follow me" (Matthew 16:24). "He that loveth father or mother more than me is not worthy of me: and he that loveth son or daughter more than me is not worthy of me" (Matthew 10:37). "If any man comes to me, and hate not his father, and mother, and wife, and children, and brethren, and sisters, yea, and his own life also, he cannot be my disciple. And whosoever doth not bear his cross, and come after me, cannot be my disciple.

So likewise, whosoever he be of you that forsaketh not all that he hath, he cannot be my disciple" (Luke 14:26-27, 33).

We can see in all this a most important and difficult choice! The call of God upon a life forces one to choose between the immediate rewards of this life and the approval of God in eternity. It is self-delusion for any Christian to imagine that the things of this world can bring satisfaction either permanently or temporarily. Peter was beginning to give himself to this dread, spiritual obscuration, for, as Christ said, "You are not setting your mind on God's interests, but man's" (Matthew 16:23, NASB).

The world is still very much with us, and it is driving itself with greater impact into our lives than ever before. How tragic that Christian young people by the millions should have become convinced that to be "with it," fashionable, relevant, a part of the "in group" is a position worth having. Millions of the people of God have become enslaved to the things of time because they did not heed the command of Scripture, "Love not the world, neither the things that are in the world. If any man love the world, the love of the Father is not in him. For all that is in the world, the lust of the flesh, and the lust of the eyes, and the pride of life, is not of the Father, but is of the world. And the world passeth away, and the lust thereof: but he that doeth the will of God abideth forever" (1 John 2:15-17).

Even in temporal things, dedication to a great purpose is a saving influence in this human life. Athletics illustrate this principle. Every four years we witness the thrilling spectacle of young Olympians winning gold medals in the arena. The winner is an infinitely happier young person as a result of the daily and painful discipline that produced his speed and endurance in competition. Who but a fool would deny that winning Olymians' lives are more desirable than that of the drug addict stumbling around alleys, hardly conscious of his own existence?

Dedication, even to a corruptible crown, produces significant dividends in this life. Dedication to the purpose of God produces infinitely greater rewards in eternity.

Having failed to prevent Christ from going to the cross, the remaining activity of Satan is to prevent Christians from fulfilling God's intention to make of us significant witnesses to what that cross means. He cannot now succeed in preventing the production of God's plan for our personal, eternal salvation. He can, however, succeed in preventing the application of that plan in the lives of my neighbors, my friends, my world of influence. He can do that by simply turning me into an ordinary, complacent, uncommitted Christian. A major segment of humanity can still be lost if Satan can succeed in neutralizing the lives of Christians, keeping them from this "spiritual extremism" of being willing to live and, perhaps, to die for Christ.

God has a wonderful plan for each Christian's life, and that plan can be beautifully fulfilled with the help of the indwelling Holy Spirit. The Christian who will take up his cross and follow Christ, the Christian who will walk in the Spirit, can see the fulfilling of that bright purpose that the Lord Jesus died to make possible. The Christian who is living up to the purpose of God for his life is a serious threat to the devil and daily is used of God to push back the powers of darkness. Satan, knowing this, constantly works to get the Christian to believe the pernicious doctrine that salvation may be worth accepting, but Christ is not worth following and obeying with the total of one's capability.

To counteract this satanic doctrine, the Word of God asks that we not only believe in Christ for salvation but that we also commit our total potential to Him in glad service. What Christ said in a dozen ways, Paul affirms, saying,

> I beseech you therefore, brethren, by the mercies of God, that ye present your bodies a living sacrifice, holy,

> acceptable unto God, which is your reasonable service.
> And be not conformed to this world: but be ye trans-
> formed by the renewing of your mind, that ye may
> prove what is that good, and acceptable, and perfect,
> will of God. (Romans 12:1-2)

In these verses, the Lord tells us as believers what results will accrue in our redeemed lives when we truly
commit ourselves to Christ. He says we will "prove," we
will bring to pass in fact, the beautiful purpose of God for
our lives. It is God's intention that we Christians be joy-
ous, capable, and successful in living this life for God. He
even tells us that we should live our lives like kings (Romans 5:17) when we truly install His principles into our
daily experience.

Much of the spiritual poverty that many Christians
experience, comes because they have believed the satanic
doctrine that was preached by Peter to the Lord Jesus:
don't take up your cross. They have consequently settled
for mediocre Christian lives, and therefore they are getting the worst of both worlds, the spiritual and the material. That is, they are being disciplined by God on the
spiritual side and laughed at by the world on the materia-
listic side. Someone has well said, "He who lives for this
world loses both this world and the world to come; whereas he who lives for the world to come gains this world in
the bargain." The Scripture establishes the principle, saying, "If in this life only we have hope in Christ, we are of
all men most miserable" (1 Corinthians 15:19).

Paul made no such mistake as investing his life in the
wrong thing. He knew of the plan of God for his life, and
he gave himself to the completion of that plan. As a result,
when the high adventure of living for God in the frame-
work of time drew to a close, Paul was able to say, "I have
fought a good fight, I have finished my course, I have kept
the faith: henceforth there is laid up for me a crown of

righteousness, which the Lord, the righteous judge, shall give me at that day: and not to me only, but unto all them also that love his appearing" (2 Timothy 4:7-8).

A life committed to Jesus Christ is the prelude to that bright moment when we stand in His presence to hear Him say, "Well done." Satanic subversion is the road to disaster, both in this life and in eternity. His infernal majesty, knowing his time is short, is working as never before to prevent us from arriving joyously in the spacious avenues of heaven. He is also working diligently to prevent us from arriving in the company of grateful brothers and sisters whom we have led to Christ. That happy fulfillment will come only if we are articulate witnesses for Him, if we take up our cross and follow Him.

We, therefore, must discern the devilish character of every alternative in life that would draw us away from the fulfillment of the plan for us that Christ died to make possible. It is imperative that we discern and successfully resist the thousand voices that come to us from every quarter, which would beguile us into wasting our lives in the Vanity Fairs of this world. Alternatives to the plan of God are finally satanic. At no time, therefore, can we let down our guard and become vulnerable to the siren song, which in one way or another says, "Don't go to the cross."

12

The Question That Remains

After we have discussed the working of Satan and especially the doctrinal base from which he operates, we face the important question, What protection do we have against satanic activity? While living in this world, we are in the presence of great moral danger. Only fools will neglect to protect themselves from its consequences.

A number of courses of action are open to the person who is in the presence of a strong and deadly enemy. Some of these may be acceptable when we are talking about merely human opposition, but most of them are unacceptable when applied to the problem of coping with Satan. We shall consider two suggestions that are unacceptable but worth considering because they have been tried by some and have probably been contemplated by most of us at one time or another. The first course of action is to flee Satan in the hope of escaping him.

Christian history indicates that the route of escaping from satanic activity has been attempted by many. Unfortunately, their attempt to escape has been without success. Monks and nuns have retreated behind the walls of monasteries and convents. Others have become hermits in their own retreats in deserts or mountains. In this way, they hoped to escape the moral infections of a corrupt civilization. In their own published confessions, they have admitted that they were still pursued by the lust of the flesh, the lust of the eye, and the pride of life. They carried sinful hearts to their hermitage, and they were unable, by mere isolation from the world, to insure themselves against defeat by the attacks of the evil one.

John Milton, in his *Areopagitica*, commented on retreat from the world most perceptibly in saying, "He that can apprehend and consider vice with all her baits and seeming pleasures, and yet abstain, and yet distinguish, and yet prefer that which is truly better, he is the true wayfaring Christian. I cannot praise a fugitive and cloistered virtue, unexercised and unbreathed, that never sallies out and sees her adversary, but slinks out of the race, where that immortal garland is to be run for, not without dust and heat."

He continued, saying, "Assuredly we bring not innocence into the world; we bring impurity much rather; that which purifies us is trial, and trial is by what is contrary. That virtue, therefore, which is but a youngling in the contemplation of evil, and knows not the utmost that vice promises to her followers, and rejects it, is but a blank virtue."

One of the most obvious facts of life is that we cannot say, "Stop the world; I want to get off." We must not, therefore, seek to escape a confrontation with evil, because, of course, such physical escape is impossible. Paul touched on this subject when writing to the Corinthians in saying, "I wrote unto you in an epistle not to company with fornicators: yet not altogether with the fornicators of this world, or with the covetous, or extortioners, or with idolaters; for then must ye needs go out of the world" (1 Corinthians 5:9-10).

"For then must ye needs go out of the world" is here stated as the obvious impossibility that it is. There is no sense in attempting to run away, for there is no place to run to. The devil will pursue us across the moat, through the gate, and into the last room of our locked castles. Escaping from the possibility of temptation in this life is a course that, being impossible, is unacceptable to a Christian. The Christian, however spiritual he may be, must still eat food, drink water, travel on roads, live under political authority; in a hundred ways, he is forced to interact with this world. It is impossible to depart physically from the presence of evil until this life is done. We must seek for an alternative.

But first we must note one exception, found in biblical advice to the young person. He is advised, "Flee . . . youthful lusts" (2 Timothy 2:22); fleshly lusts war against the soul (1 Peter 2:11). While we cannot bodily flee Satan in most situations, youthful lusts are the exception. We are here being warned that youthful lusts, especially sexual desires, are powerful forces in the young, immature heart. Don't rationalize, the Scripture teaches. Don't stay in its presence; get out! At times, even the courageous must run for their lives. Even some adults, flirting with their second childhood, are well advised in the same direction.

But, most of the time, when faced with the larger world of satanic temptation, we cannot flee. What then? Another tack that is practiced by many and is also unacceptable, is negotiation and compromise with evil.

"If you can't fight 'em, join 'em" is the way the saying goes. By this standard, the victory of evil is thought of as being so inevitable that we have no possibility except to go along with the course of this world. In each of our experiences, we come across this view stated in a thousand ways. Many believe, almost as an article of faith, that you cannot be a good politician without "rising above" your principles. The car dealer must turn the odometers back, and the policeman has to be on the take in order to make it. "There is a little larceny in each of us," the cynics say; "so, why fight it?" The view of many, therefore, is that we have no alternative except to strike up a friendship with this world in order to succeed in the midst of the human scene.

This, of course, is an attractive but always unsuccessful game. This is why the Bible warns us, "Whosoever therefore will be a friend of the world is the enemy of God" (James 4:4). The Christian is called upon to be a discerning person. He must live in the midst of a world that has the disease of original sin, but he must not become infected by it. The Christian must walk the tightrope between powerful political, moral, and spiritual alternatives. This is one of the aspects of the Christian life that makes it exciting, the challenge of walking between the forbidden alternatives of asceticism and concession.

What course of action is recommended, indeed *commanded*, to the Christian in this world? *Resistance.* We are clearly told, "Resist the devil, and he will flee from you" (James 4:7). We are protagonists in a spiritual warfare, in which we are to "be strong in the Lord, and in the power of his might." Paul's earnest admonition to the Christian "soldier" gives us most helpful instructions as to how to equip ourselves to resist the devil and to fight the good fight of faith. We are advised to "put on the whole armour of God, that ye may be able to stand against the wiles of the devil" (Ephesians 6:1).

In talking about the whole armor of God, Paul implies that there is adequate equipment available for us to function effectively in the military conflict called *life*. He offers several areas of provision, presented as pieces of armor, that the Christian has available to him, which will help him to battle adequately. If we are poorly equipped in any of these areas, we will be vulnerable to damaging satanic activity from an unguarded quarter. Only spiritual irresponsibility will ignore the provision that God has made for capability while campaigning in the treacherous warfare of this life.

And what a warfare it is! Each day that we live, without exception, we will operate in a no-man's land of angry

guns and exploding rockets. Our courage will be ever test-
ed and our strength taxed to the ninth degree. Our loves,
loyalties, hopes, and fears are all components in the great
battle of life. We must steel ourselves for the supreme test,
allowing no shocking sight or sound to deter us from the
only goal: victory. The enemy *must* be defeated. Christ
must prevail. We must equip ourselves adequately for the
struggle. Our equipment has been provided.

The first piece of equipment is the girdle of truth.
"Stand therefore, having your loins girt about with truth"
(Ephesians 6:14a). So again, we are reminded that the
first problem of the world is the problem of truth. Our
world's first need is to know truth. Men are asking as never before, What is truth? They are seeking, usually in
vain, for a sure foundation on which a system of faith can
be built.

The Christian has no such problem, for he holds
within his hands the ultimate source of truth, the Bible. It
follows that the greatest need of the Christian in our present age is to return to an intense and detailed study of the
pages of sacred Scripture. This is the imperative for any
Christian who would be equipped to live this life successfully. The man of God can be mature, thoroughly furnished unto all good works, only as he gives himself to a
study of the Scripture that alone is profitable for doctrine,
reproof, correction, and instruction in righteousness.

We see the positive and negative illustrations of this
fact on every hand. The Christian who becomes strong
and capable, characterized by spiritual growth and leadership, is the one who has an ever expanding knowledge of
the Word of God. He moves from strength to strength,
ever climbing from cowardice to capability, from vacilla-
tion to clear and purposeful courage. Fellowship, activity,
and service may all be fine, but a knowledge of the Word
of God is the absolute imperative, it is the source of Christian capability.

The converse is obvious. The Christian who is ignorant of sound doctrine is easily defeated. His faith flags and zeal fades. Why? He has slipped away from a daily study of Scripture. One can never find motivation or capability in mere service; he must find it in constant attention to the foundation of his life, the Word of God.

Our present religious scene gives us corporate illustrations of this as well. A new thing has happened in our time. Historically, true Christianity has usually been the little flock. The gospel seemed to embody itself in small, beleaguered groups of the faithful. Those who forsook the faith seemed to be the ones who prospered. Now, the disillusionment of our age has somewhat changed that. Churches and organizations that have stayed true to the fundamental teaching of Scripture are the ones that are prospering. They have experienced growth, financial success, and wide influence. The largest Sunday schools, the most sacrificially giving memberships, the greatest numbers of people are in the constituencies of those evangelists, pastors, and Christian leaders, who stand unashamedly for the inerrancy and infallibility of Scripture. The call to "preach the Word" is not only the basis of divine blessing, it becomes, when other foundations fail, the only method for producing lasting response. The individual or the organization that would stand against satanic opposition in a world like this is one that is first and always girded about with truth.

Note also that this passage admonishes us to have our "loins" girded about with truth. In the Scripture, the loins represent the emotions. Satanic temptation, whether toward indulgence, sexual lust, or mere aesthetic fulfillment, is basically an emotional temptation. Our present age is more emotionally oriented than most. It constantly falls for clever satanic appeals to the lust of the flesh, which are based on human emotion and can only be resisted with truth. The vulnerable loins of our present age are sadly in need of the protection of the girdle of truth.

It is obvious, then, that to deny truth, objective value,

is to produce the destruction of mankind. A return to the truth of Holy Scripture is the only possible key to the survival of society.

We are also admonished to take to ourselves the breastplate of righteousness (Ephesians 6:14*b*). The world was made by a God whose basic attribute is holiness. We each have violated that holiness. We "have sinned, and come short of the glory of God" (Romans 3:23). We have violated the dictates of absolute truth. It is our individual moral faults that make it possible for Satan to gain the advantage of us. We will be unprotected from his fearful ravages unless we take to ourselves that blessed provision of the breastplate of righteousness.

And how shall we do this? Shall we achieve righteousness by our own works, our own doings, our own religion? The answer, of course, is no. We are disqualified from any kind of righteousness based on our own activity, our pathetic attempts to please God. From whence, then, comes righteousness that will be a source of our defense against the activity of Satan?

The answer to this imperative need is in the Christian doctrine of justification by faith. "Now to him that worketh is the reward not reckoned of grace, but of debt. But to him that worketh not, but believeth on him that justifieth the ungodly, his faith is counted for righteousness. Even as David also describeth the blessedness of the man, unto whom God imputeth righteousness without works" (Romans 4:4-6).

Righteousness without works, apart from our own activity—what a wonderful gift! This marvelous justification from God comes to us by faith in Jesus Christ "who of God is made unto us wisdom, and righteousness, and sanctification, and redemption" (1 Corinthians 1:30).

We must also note that the breastplate of righteousness as a present possession implies the necessity of us walking in righteous response to the will of God. "He that saith he abideth in him ought himself also so to walk, even as he walked" (1 John 2:6). The happy course of the Christian life is that we are to perfect holiness in the fear of God (2 Corinthians 7:1). No Christian can hope to be a good soldier unless he is following the path of progressive sanctification. His progress in the perfecting of holiness in his life makes it decreasingly possible for Satan to gain the advantage of him. He will be protected from the devastating damage that the evil one can do when he is walking in the confidence before God, which comes from an uncondemned heart (1 John 3:21).

This passage also suggests that we have our feet shod with "the preparation of the gospel of peace." We are to equip ourselves to become articulate witnesses for Christ. This form of warfare in which we interact with this world is that, as ambassadors for Christ, we press the message of the good news upon people who do not know God.

The adequate witness for Christ is the one who takes to himself the highest possible degree of understanding that he can accumulate about the needs of other human beings and the answer that is found to those needs in the Word of God. The expression, "He that winneth souls is wise" may not only suggest the nature but also the preparation of the soul-winner. The person who witnesses unwisely may do a great deal of spiritual harm in the life of a person whom he attempts to reach for the Savior. Conversely, the prepared witness, who thoroughly understands the gospel of the grace of God, will experience the greater degree of success in his ambassadorship for the Savior.

That does not mean that we are simply "used of God" without respect to our degree of preparation. Rather, it clearly teaches us that we are to study, think, plan, analyze, and comprehend the needs of men, the gospel answer, and the place where we fit into that answer. No two people are alike. It is probable, therefore, that no two lost sinners will be won by the identical recitation of the gospel. Little books or short courses may be fine, but nothing takes the place of an adequate and scholarly preparation of the gospel.

The gospel of the grace of God is at once a simple and a profound message. It will never be adequately represented by those who leaf through a few quick pages in the hope of producing a considered and eternal decision. The good soldier is one who has prepared himself in the gospel of peace.

We must also take to ourselves the shield of faith. Faith is looking at the things that are not seen as against the things that are seen. Faith is believing, to the point of personal certainty, in the substance of things hoped for and the evidence of things not seen. Faith is distinct from sight, from experience, from empirical proof. We will never retain the motivation to "keep on keeping on" for the Lord unless we are inspired by the perennial energy that issues from our faith. This provocative passage of Scripture teaches us that it is by faith that we are able to resist the fiery darts of the wicked.

Satan has many darts that he may hurl in our direction. The primary one is discouragement. Repeatedly in the Word of God, we are admonished not to be weary in well doing. We are told that we will reap if we faint not. The only defense against the discouragement that would cause us to faint and retire from the battle before we have effectively confronted the enemy is our faith. At a given point, we may not be able to prove that we are succeeding, or even surviving, but we know this to be the case by faith.

There is no external, human standard by which we can be sure that we are adequately serving God. The large crowds, the big buildings, the applause, the letters of commendation, the adequate financing, these are all helpful but constitute no final evidence of the blessing of God upon our work. We will be saved from discouragement, not by the presence of any of these human things, but by the possession of faith. At times, we will be abased; at times, we will abound. We must learn to be enriched; we must also learn to suffer loss. No proposition is more foolish, indeed more satanic, than to estimate that the blessing of God can be measured by money in the bank or the applause of the crowd. There is no human measure of success. There is only the measure of faith. "We look not at the things which are seen, but at the things which are not seen: for the things which are seen are temporal; but the things which are not seen are eternal" (2 Corinthians 4:18).

We can quench all the fiery darts of the wicked if we do not grow weary in the battle, if we do not succumb to the dart of discouragement. We will only prevail when protected by the shield of faith.

The helmet of salvation is the imperative armament. The soldier who is not really a Christian at all will quickly succumb to a blow on the head. The helmet of salvation, the sure knowledge that we ourselves are personally saved, is a most strategic armament indeed. In today's religious society, many wear the fancy trappings of ecclesiastical ornamentation, but they are unprotected by the helmet of salvation.

The whole story of being a successful soldier begins when one has the assurance within his heart that he knows Jesus Christ as his personal Savior. There are occasions when we must heed the admonition of Paul to the Corinthians, "Examine yourself, whether ye be in the faith" (2 Corinthians 13:5).

Many a preacher and not a few other kinds of religious leaders have come to the place in their threadbare ministries where they realize that they have never really started the Christian life at all. They have not personally come to Christ. They have not exercised faith in the Son of God. Many also are the followers of the Christian religion who have never realized that Christianity is not religion at all but a relationship with the Son of God. Personal salvation has escaped them. How wonderful has been their testimony when they turned to Christ and believed the gospel. The helmet of salvation is the one protection from certain death at the hands of the evil one.

We are finally invited to take into our hands the sword of the Spirit, which is the Word of God. This is a call to learn to use the Word of God as an offensive weapon against the wiles of the devil. To know the Bible to the place where it satisfies *us* is one thing. To be well versed enough in Scripture to use it as a weapon in a conflict against Satan is quite another. A small degree of understanding of the Bible, mixed with faith, will produce salvation. No such small understanding, however, will produce Christian capability in the great battle that we now face in our present age. The successful soldier, then, is the one who becomes knowledgeable to the point of mastery of Scripture. He is the one who is "ready always to give an answer to every man that asketh [him] a reason of the hope" that is in him (1 Peter 3:15). He is the one who can stand against a subtle foe and give "place by subjection, no, not for an hour; that the truth of the gospel might continue with you" (Galatians 2:5). He is set for the "defense and confirmation of the gospel" (Philippians 1:7). He is skillful in the use of the Word of God.

The unfortunate problem of our present age is that these individuals are somewhat rare. Too many Christians have settled for the simple outline produced on their denominational mimeograph machine and have developed little knowledge beyond this. We must assure ourselves that there is no religious syndicate, no organization, that has a corner on the knowledge of Scripture. Each individual is called upon to know the Word of God for himself. Indeed, no ministry is doing its job unless it produces individual competence in Scripture. Too many organizations are merely producing a limp mass of spiritual dependents, saints who are not equipped to study the Bible for themselves. They must ever be propped up by their spiritual gurus, never coming to the place of personal doctrinal expertise.

No ministry is successful unless it produces independent capability in the lives of those whom it reaches. The
individual who comes to the place of independent capability, who enjoys the blessing of God in spiritual growth to
the extent that he is "combat ready" is the one who medi-
tates day and night in the Scriptures.

While evangelical Christianity has grown commend-
ably in these years, it still possesses a major problem,
spiritual vulnerability. Dozens of well-promoted cults and
sects are experiencing a field day, in that they are able to
beguile thousands of immature and naive Christians into
their simplistic and pseudo-authoritarian religions. Spiritual carnage has resulted in the lives of multiplied thousands of babes in Christ, for want of a development in the
use of the sword of the Spirit, the Word of God. They have
been subverted by Satan into sweet-sounding but false religions, only because of their lack of biblical knowledge.

Indeed, this is becoming a most serious problem
within the church. Ours has been a generation of evangelism. We must rejoice in the millions who have been won
for Christ through the wide dissemination of the gospel.
Today's media have made it possible for the eternal message to be brought to major segments of the population of
the world. The seed has fallen on good ground; germinat-
ing, it has sprouted with promise of producing mature
Christian lives. The problem is that the wide dissemination of seed-sowing evangelism has been but fractionally
matched by an equally wide teaching of sound, biblical
doctrine. The consequence is that among the masses who
claim to know Christ, there are relative few who are able
to give a reason for the hope that is in them.

The presence of spiritual quickening along with the
absence of sound doctrine has created the great problem
in the church of our present age, cultic vulnerability. Like
the Galatians, who began well in the faith but soon became re-enslaved to the law of Moses, Christians today are
in danger of being victimized by one of the many clever

systems that claim to be the full or the complete version of Christianity. Only a solid program of Bible study can prevent the spiritually naive from being beguiled away from the simplicity that is in Christ. Satan, our tireless enemy, may yet have his way with many who are moving joyously now through the spiritual springtime of their lives. The heat of summer may quench the sparkling foundation of early faith because it did not renew itself with the water of the Word.

Having equipped ourselves as good soldiers of the cross, we are encouraged toward a final activity in this spiritual warfare that is our life. The soldier is called upon most earnestly to watch and to pray. "Praying always with all prayer and supplication in the Spirit, and watching thereunto with all perseverance and supplication for all saints" (Ephesians 6:18). Again, the call is that we must be sober and vigilant, because we daily face the adversary of our lives. Prayerful watching, or watchful prayer, must become our diligent and daily activity. No one ever develops the knowledge or human competence that brings him to the place that alleviates the need for prayer. No one ever reaches the spiritual cloister where he needs no longer to carefully watch. To watch is to constantly examine the world in the midst of which we walk. It is that horizontal wariness for want of which the Christian may receive a wound from an unsurveyed direction. Prayer is that vertical upreach by which we receive from our God the wisdom and the strength to walk and to watch.

The lesson is clear that neither necessity in the Christian life must be neglected. The pietists would have us only pray and the pragmatists would have us only watch. "Be spiritual," says the one; "be practical," says the other. The perceptive Christian believes neither view as the single course for him. Rather, he embraces both. The clouds as well as the cobblestones are familiar territory for him. He knows how to guardedly breathe the murk of the valleys as well as to exultantly inhale the purer drafts at the mountaintops. His oath of loyalty to his Commander includes the possibility of service on the snows of the mountains or in the fetid valley swamps.

In whatever circumstances, he watches and he prays, for he knows that he is being relentlessly stalked by Satan, his determined foe. Transforming himself into a roaring lion, an angel of light, a grievous wolf, or even a loving friend, his enemy is the fateful hunter so long as this human life shall last—which is not forever. We are taught that the day is coming in which Satan and his cohorts shall be cast into the lake of fire, forever banished from the presence of God and from the possibility of plaguing the steps of the Christian. It is then that the long and tortuous battles of time will be past. Then shall we understand, as we do not understand now, that the wounds and pains sustained in our mortal struggle against the power of his infernal majesty were indeed the allowances of a loving God.

We shall understand then that conflict, not isolation, was the best kind of life to live. We will comprehend then the reason God allowed the devil to do his worst against us.

Then we shall understand what faith alone teaches us now, that Satan's worst was necessary to produce our best, and that for eternity.

Moody Press, a ministry of the Moody Bible Institute, is designed for education, evangelization, and edification. If we may assist you in knowing more about Christ and the Christian life, please write us without obligation: Moody Press, c/o MLM, Chicago, Illinois 60610.